Images in Social Media

Categorization and Organization of Images and Their Collections

Synthesis Lectures on Information Concepts, Retrieval, and Services

Editor
Gary Marchionini, *University of North Carolina at Chapel Hill*

Synthesis Lectures on Information Concepts, Retrieval, and Services publishes short books on topics pertaining to information science and applications of technology to information discovery, production, distribution, and management. Potential topics include: data models, indexing theory and algorithms, classification, information architecture, information economics, privacy and identity, scholarly communication, bibliometrics and webometrics, personal information management, human information behavior, digital libraries, archives and preservation, cultural informatics, information retrieval evaluation, data fusion, relevance feedback, recommendation systems, question answering, natural language processing for retrieval, text summarization, multimedia retrieval, multilingual retrieval, and exploratory search.

vii

Images in Social Media: Categorization and Organization of Images and Their
Collections Susanne Ørnager and Haakon Lund

ISBN: 978-3-031-01186-3 print
ISBN: 978-3-031-02314-9 ebook
ISBN: 978-3-031-00221-2 hardcover

DOI 10.1007/978-3-031-02314-9

A Publication in the Springer series
SYNTHESIS LECTURES ON INFORMATION CONCEPTS, RETRIEVAL, AND SERVICES, #62
Series Editors: Gary Marchionini, University of North Carolina, Chapel Hill

Series ISSN: 1947-945X Print   1947-9468 Electronic

Images in Social Media

Categorization and Organization of Images and Their Collections

Susanne Ørnager and Haakon Lund
University of Copenhagen

SYNTHESIS LECTURES ON INFORMATION CONCEPTS, RETRIEVAL, AND SERVICES #62

ABSTRACT

This book focuses on the methodologies, organization, and communication of digital image collection research that utilizes social media content. ("Image" is here understood as a cultural, conventional, and commercial—stock photo—representation.) The lecture offers expert views that provide different interpretations of images and their potential implementations. Linguistic and semiotic methodologies as well as eye-tracking research are employed to both analyze images and comprehend how humans consider them, including which salient features generally attract viewers' attention.

This literature review covers image—specifically photographic—research since 2005, when major social media platforms emerged. A citation analysis includes an overview of co-citation maps that demonstrate the nexus of image research literature and the journals in which they appear. Eye tracking tests whether scholarly templates focus on the proper features of an image, such as people, objects, time, etc., and if a prescribed theme affects the eye movements of the observer. The results may point to renewed requirements for building image search engines. As it stands, image management already requires new algorithms and a new understanding that involves text recognition and very large database processing.

The aim of this book is to present different image research areas and demonstrate the challenges image research faces. The book's scope is, by necessity, far from comprehensive, since the field of digital image research does not cover fake news, image manipulation, mobile photos, etc.; these issues are very complex and need a publication of their own. This book should primarily be useful for students in library and information science, psychology, and computer science.

KEYWORDS

images, social media, image tags, academic image domains, image facets, image indexing, image guidelines, image retrieval, image literature review, PRISMA, Grounded Theory, eye-tracking, salient image features, test image templates, image citation analysis, image management, text recognition, image literacy

Contents

Preface

Social media has focused much on pictures since its inception in 2005, and the amount of images on social media is overwhelming. It is impossible to be certain, but the number of images on social media can be counted in the billions. According to Search Engine Watch (2016), approximately 80 million images are uploaded every day to Instagram alone. What can be done with this titanic number of images? Do we strive for systems that can provide us with systematic access to all available images? Or, are we working toward systems where only a fraction of the available images is also retrievable?

Before the invention of social media, most research literature was concerned with classification schemes and their utilization for indexing and retrieving images as well as the improvement of these systems. Digitization of images began in the 1980s, and apart from storage problems that were resolved in the 1990s, the emphasis was on the amendment of taxonomies and on offering pictures in different sizes, where thumbnail recognition was frequently used because it provides a quick overview of many images. Query by Image Content (QBIC) is an approach that researches ways to extend and improve query methods for image databases. QBIC allows queries on large image and video databases based on example images, user-constructed sketches and drawings, selected color and texture patterns, camera and object motion, and other graphical information. However, none of these approaches have been successful solutions, although they have led the way for today's achievements.

After the launch of social media, experts realized that they could now test various indexing and retrieval methods in a new and cheap fashion using social networks, where they distinguish between controlled indexing based on classification techniques and uncontrolled indexing labeled tags. Several network providers use the successor to QBIC, known as Content-Based Image Retrieval (CBIR), where the contents are color, shape of a particular region in the picture, and texture features. However, these aspects only cover factual information. A picture can have different interpretations and meanings to different people even within the same domain, and the description and retrieval may depend on the user's situation and the research questions the scholar is facing. These interpretations, meanings, and descriptions need to be clarified before digitization.

In this book, we focus on what has been studied by academics and published in research papers concerning images in the digital age. We present a citation analysis to illustrate on which background the scholars build their research and if the history of image studies hamper new digital approaches. In the 1930s, groundbreaking research on eye movements and the connection between visual stimuli and cognitive processes was conducted. This research investigated users' areas of interests, i.e., measuring where the users' eyes dwell for a longer period of time on an image. Eye movement research still can offer a deeper understanding of our cognitive processes while also showing promising results in identifying the semantic structure of images by analyzing eye movements. Big data is available and data is important; however, data must be used with a strategy, and our smartest machines are still blind, so to take a picture is not the same as seeing a picture. We have to teach the computer to see like a human, which is more than factual CBIR. We want the computer to understand context and semantics from both the images and natural language synthesis, e.g., to dissect images into drops of similar colors and then use these drops as words of a visual vocabulary, i.e., automatic image indexing.

The target audience for this book is students in library information science, psychology, and computer science, but it is also relevant for people working in various fields and the interested non-professional who wishes to have up-to-date knowledge of photographic research.

Susanne Ørnager and Haakon Lund
October 2017

Acknowledgments

We are grateful to the many colleagues who have contributed to this work in various ways, particularly Ragnhild Riis, Mette Sandbye, Mette Kia Krabbe Meyer, Louise Broch, Hans Dam Christensen, and Lorna Elizabeth Wildgaard.

Susanne Ørnager and Haakon Lund
October 2017

Abbreviations

AAT = Art & Architecture Thesaurus

AHCI = Arts and Humanities Citation Index

AOI = Areas of Interest

CBIR = Content-based Image Retrieval

CCO = Cataloging Cultural Objects: A Guide to Describing Cultural Works and Their Images

COCO = Common Objects in COntext

CoPhIR = Content-based Photo Image Retrieval

DCNN = Deep Convolutional Neural Networks

DLP = Deep Learning Paradigm

FGC = Flickr General Collection

GT = Grounded Theory

HOPR = Hierarchy for Online Photograph Representation model

IPTC = International Press Telecommunications Council

IR = Information Retrieval

LC = Library of Congress

LCP = Library of Congress's Photo-stream

LCSH = Library of Congress Subject Headings

LIS = Library and Information Science

LISA = Library and Information Science Abstracts

LISTA = Library, Information Science, and Technology Abstracts

LoC = Library of Congress

MIR = Music Information Retrieval System

PRISMA = Preferred Reporting Items for Systematic Reviews and Meta-Analyses Guidelines

SAM = Self-Assessment Manikin

SCI = Science Citation Index

SD = Semantic Differential

SIGGRAPH =Special Interest Group on Computer GRAPHics and Interactive Techniques

SSCI = Social Science Citation Index

TED = Technology, Entertainment, Design

TGM = Thesaurus for Graphic Materials

TREC = Text REtrieval Conference

UADs = User-Assigned Descriptors

UHDL = University of Houston Digital Library

CHAPTER   1

Introduction and Iconic Language for Images

The aim of this book is to present a literary review on image research since the onset of social media in 2005 and outline the image challenges in the digital age. The term *image* here is narrowed down to photography and image, and *picture*, *photography*, and *photo* are synonyms in this book. This book is primarily for students in library and information science, psychology, and computer science although it is also relevant for people working with images in various fields and the interested nonprofessional who wishes to have up-to-date knowledge of photographic research and prognosis for future purposes. We are well aware that the main factor behind the enormous number of stored photographs on social media is due to the presence of smart phones in everyday life. This has made the capture of events much easier compared to earlier analog technologies, but it has also complicated the questions of how to organize and retrieve photos. A number of solutions to these issues are available, but users are asked to make decisions about the management of photos. In the future this may evolve into practical solutions for everyday utilization. What the huge amount of photos on social media now offers is a set of test collections for research into applying different results for image indexing and retrieval either manually or automatically. The authors' scope here is therefore far from being comprehensive, and the book does not cover fake news, image manipulation, etc. as these issues are very complex and need a publication of their own.

Social media is often used to describe services such as Twitter, Facebook, Instagram, Flickr, Snapshot, and others. Obar and Wildman (2015) amalgamate several definitions and come up with four consistencies about social media services.

1. Social media services are (currently) Web 2.0 Internet-based applications.

2. User-generated content is the lifeblood of social media.

3. Individuals and groups create user-specific profiles for a site or app designed and maintained by a social media service.

4. Social media services facilitate the development of social networks online by connecting a profile with those of other individuals and/or groups.

Although the list above is a statement of intent, a working definition of social media based on the four commonalities has been suggested as "*web-based communication tools that enable people to interact with each other by both sharing and consuming information*" (Nations, 2017).

There is a difference between social and professional media since the first is described as a communication tool and the latter is mostly meant for research or commercial use. However, new ways are exposed with the appearance of social media since it provides possibilities for scholars to try out different tools in a less expensive way.

What meaning does an image have for social media?

Mette Kia Krabbe Meyer, Royal Danish Library

Even if an actual image seems to become less important, it is still central in the social media lives we are leading. Critics point to the superficiality and beautification in play on social media but everybody at the same time acknowledges image sharing as a social kit. Sharing images, whether of shared experiences or individual ones, strengthens a sense of community. A hundred years ago we sent photographs by mail to share moments from our lives; now we are sharing instantly from our telephones. During the last decade we have seen how certain images taken by amateurs have gone viral. Some of them have been taken in war or during political conflicts around the world and, generally speaking, we see social media gaining importance as a news forum and amateur photography gaining importance as well. But, again, it is very hard to speak about the image or photography as such. Photocritics have been pointing to the diversity of the medium and to the need for us to specify which photographs we are talking about. Also, when it comes to images spread on social media there are many different types—not only images taken by amateurs but also by professionals in domains like press, advertising, etc. An interesting development has been the return of the montage as a critical tool. When Siegfried Kracauer and Walter Benjamin wrote about photographs in 1927 and 1931, respectively, artists such as Hannah Höch and John Heartfield had been cutting out photographs and gluing them together as new critical images for some duration. Today, the population at large digitally recreates photographs of politicians, actors, and others and circulates them. In this way, a new kind of critical montage has been developed.

Mette Kia Krabbe Meyer is a Ph.D. and a senior researcher in the Collections of Maps, Prints, and Photographs at the Royal Danish Library. She is responsible for accession, registration, research, and communication in the image collection. She received her Ph.D. in Danish interwar photography from the University of Copenhagen in 2004. Recently, she has been in charge of digitizing the library's First World War collections as well as images of the former Danish West Indies Colony. She has co-curated the exhibitions Lay Down Your Arms (2014) and Blind Spot and Images of the Danish West Indies Colony (2017). She is currently a board member in LFF (National Association for the Conservation of Photo and Film): http://fotoogfilm.org.

In 1839, the daguerreotype—the first successful photographic process—was commercially introduced and this is the date generally accepted as the birth year of physical photography. The daguerreotype is accurate, detailed, and sharp, has a mirror-like surface, and is very fragile. Although daguerreotypes are rare they appear scattered in institutional and private collections all over the world. Since 1839 both professional and private photos have advanced and today sites and apps such as Flickr, Instagram, and Facebook are used daily by many millions of people to circulate their pictures.

Since the invention of photography, photos have been shared and utilized as background for storytelling and as extended memories. Family photo albums are treasured by many. Today, although the amount of digital images is overwhelming, we still have photo albums. Many companies offer software for making digital and paper albums and one can still find ways to share holidays and birthdays with family and friends. Images load on our mobile phones and are found on different social media sites generating a pile of photos that may be used again—if they can be retrieved.

Photography or photos are handled by researchers in such institutions as libraries, archives, museums, various organizations, stock photo bureaus, and commercial offices. Photos are deposited and accessed, which require collection-management policies, i.e., common rules for storage and retrieval. The photos are part of our nation's history and the memory of the world. Over the years, researchers have developed and refined image indexing and retrieval tools. Images, however, have been associated with what can be called "special collections," i.e., collections for users with special interests. As images used to belong to "collection minorities" they have not been considered as interesting as document collections. This situation drastically changed with digital development and now the image is an information resource like any other resource stored in any social network/media, database, or website.

What meaning does an image have for social media?

Mette Sandbye, University of Copenhagen

As the meaning implies, it is about social communication and here photography plays an important role—together with texts in many formats, of course. We depict, share, and thereby also negotiate, play with, and try to understand ourselves and our daily way of living visually, via social media. Let's take such a thing as the selfie. Some have argued that this is a superficial, or even dangerous, way of depicting and sharing your "ideal" self. But as a phenomenon it must be understood much more nuanced. I would suggest to see the selfie as a part of a psychological and philosophical process of understanding and exploring identity in a complicated modern world.

Mette Sandbye is a Professor of Photography Studies and since 2012 has been the Head of the Department of Arts and Cultural Studies at the University of Copenhagen. She currently researches the relationship between amateur photography and collective history since the 1960s. She has written extensively on photography and contemporary art for more than 20 years. In 2010 she was a member of the Hasselblad Award committee, and from 2007–2011 she was a member of the Danish Arts Council, board of visual arts. Her latest book is *Digital Snaps: The New Face of Photography* (Larson and Sandbye, 2014).

1.1   ICONIC LANGUAGE FOR IMAGES

For some years, research papers have focused on varoius methods concerning image storage and retrieval. Articles concerning Content-Based Image Retrieval (CBIR), a machine description of visual media where low-level features such as color and size are indexed and retrieved automatically, illustrate one method. Other methods are about systems concentrating on the concept of photos and determining what a viewer observes in an image as well as the meaning of an image. All methods utilize experiments to consolidate their views.

There are few rules guiding the indexing and retrieval of private pictures most likely because the need for guidelines is not overwhelming. However, professional images have always been categorized by rules either in verbal form or codified for retrieval. With social media new means are available for testing regulations, and with digital development new tools can be examined.

1.2   THE MEANING OF AN IMAGE

The French semiotics scholar Roland Barthes (1915–1980) established the field of semiology (Chandler, 2002) to examine all forms of expression including the pictorial. In his terminology, Barthes uses the set of concepts *denotation/connotation* (Barthes, 1964). Briefly, *denotation* can be explained as the neutral expressions of the signs which are, however, a product of the meaning assigned to them by a given system of language within a given culture group. *Connotation* is briefly defined as meanings relating to feelings, associations, and aesthetic impressions. An example of a denotation would be "a fire" or "a girl", and the connotation for this would be "freedom", "heroin", and "Joan of Arc". On the basis of advertising photographs, Barthes concludes that the photograph conveys three messages: a linguistic one; a literal one; and a symbolic one. The *linguistic* message lies in the text, if any, accompanying the photograph. The purpose of this is to emphasize the meaning of the photograph. As a photograph often holds many meanings, the linguistic message will anchor the content, that is, pin down one single meaning. On the denotative level, the anchoring acts as an answer to the question "what is this?" The *literal* message has a purely descriptive function as it identifies the objects photographed. The *symbolic* message belongs to the connotation level. It reflects the subjective element of the photograph—the individual or cultural experience and knowledge.

We claim that in a photo the denotative level can be subdivided into a linguistic and a literal level while the connotative level only has one subgroup, the symbolic level (see Figure 1.1).

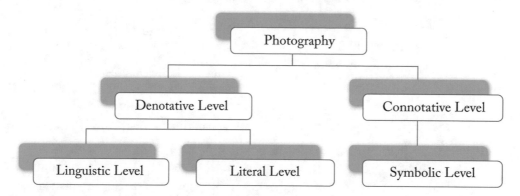

Figure 1.1: Different messages in a photograph (Ørnager, 1997).

According to Barthes (1964; 1969; 1980), the documentary and press photos are characterized by displaying reality in the form of events or objects which may be verbalized. Furthermore, such photographs are a subjective interpretation of reality and obviously a very small part of that. It may present some difficulty verbalizing the space surrounding the photograph. A simplified definition is that the photograph has a literal message and a symbolic message, whereas the literal message has a descriptive function (the symbolic message is partly subjective) (Ørnager, 1997).

Why are photographs interesting?

Mette Kia Krabbe Meyer

About a hundred years ago, the German cultural critic Siegfried Kracauer, in his article "Photography" (1927), stated that the world had "taken on a photographic face". The number of photographs in newspapers, magazines, on posters, etc. was increasing, and people experienced that their world picture was not only made up of what they actually saw themselves, but increasingly by photographs in print. And to Kracauer this meant a change in behavior as people individually and collectively acted differently in the presence of cameras. Today, our world picture is highly mediated, and no one can imagine what a world without photographs would look like. A decade ago, Kracauer (Mehring, 1997) and his contemporary Walter Benjamin (2015) called attention not only to the massive spread of photography but also to the danger of perceiving images as objective and somehow truthful pictures of the world. In the 1930s, the two were among the first to develop a critical examination of photographs including an analysis of their aesthetic and political contexts. Today, as photography is still evolving technically and aesthetically and is part of our private and public sphere in ever-changing ways, we are on an ongoing mission to understand photography's impact on our view of the world.

Text analysis has a long history, and as part of literary history, and history more broadly, textual sources are analyzed, their viewpoints laid out, and put into context. Images and especially photographs, with their mechanical realism, are still very often taken to be neutral windows to the world. Gradually, this is changing as we discover time and again the subjectiveness of photography. But seen from an academic point of view, much work is needed on the conceptual frameworks for understanding photographs and their cultural embeddedness. A photograph from the Danish Caribbean a hundred years ago—which I am currently working with—is not a direct entry to the past. It's a representation in a certain medium, made by someone with specific equipment at a specific moment and used, seen, and interpreted by others later on. When you talk about manipulation of a photograph, you somehow assume that it is pure from the start. When you are handling a text, you experience from the beginning that it is constructed.

To the naked eye a photograph is not reality but an analogical reproduction of reality; however, a second meaning or a supplementary message is usually developed when we look at a photo. Barthes (1961) refers to this as the "culture" of the society receiving the message. Its signs are gestures, attitudes, expressions, colors, or effects, endowed with certain meanings by virtue of the practice of this "culture". The photographic "copy" is taken as the pure and simple denotation of reality. To find the code of connotation could be to isolate elements of the photograph from the reader's cultural situation but this task will take us a long time indeed. Another way is to let the reading depend on the reader's culture and knowledge of the world. Actually, a good press photo, and even photos appearing on social networks and websites, make ready play with the supposed knowledge of its readers.

Why are photographs interesting?

Mette Sandbye

The answer to that question could be extremely long since photography is a really complicated praxis as well as image type. But to put it shortly, first I would underline two aspects: a philosophical one and a social one. Philosophically, or rather phenomenologically, photography was invented in early modernity where the traditional concepts of "time" and "space" are being challenged by new inventions such as the telegraph, the radio, the car, and later the airplane, etc. Fundamentally, photographs connect us with "what was". To understand yourself as a human being it is important to be able to grasp your existence as an existence in time—from birth until death—as phenomenologists from Henri Bergson to Heidegger to Ricoeur have put forward. Photography helps us to fixate time and thereby reflect on, and better understand, ourselves living in time and to a certain degree in a given space as well. Or, they can make us see and understand spaces all over the world, spaces we have never seen with our own eyes. Ever since its invention, photography has served as a kind of tool for the modern individual to understand ourselves as people with a past, a present, and a future.

Second, the social aspects of photography are very relevant, and have always been. But it is an aspect that the invention of the digital camera and the Internet have highlighted. Photography is about sharing images, making or maintaining a visual but at the same time highly social contact and communication with others, for instance by documenting your daily life as well as the most important ritual events of your life and sharing it with others. Earlier on this was done in the physical family photo album; today it is mostly done via the Internet.

The German-American art historian Erwin Panofsky (1892–1968) worked with the symbols and iconography in art. Panofsky identified an overflow of hidden symbols in Renaissance art. Anecdotally, it was claimed that Panofsky was the one coaching art historians about this theory. True or not, Panofsky and his circle claimed that it is important to consider different layers when one examines Renaissance art. The content of an image is an essential part of image analyses. Panofsky describes three levels of meaning in a work of art (Panofsky, 1962). He uses the terms *pre-iconography* for the primary level, *iconography* for the secondary level, and *iconology* for the third level. Panofsky assumes that for the "reader" to be equipped to explain the first level it is necessary for him/her to be able to describe the motifs on the basis of his/hers practical experience and be familiar with objects and events. The iconographical analysis presupposes much more than that familiarity with objects and events, which we acquire by practical experience. It presumes a familiarity with specific themes or concepts as transmitted through literary sources. The third level involves the elucidation of intrinsic meaning or contents, i.e., the symbolic values or familiarity with the essential tendencies of the human mind (Ørnager, 1997).

Panofsky's theory about analysis of ways in which one perceives and interprets experience was adapted first by the information science specialist Karen Markey (1983) in her analysis of representational images and later by the library researcher Sara Shatford (1986). The latter suggests a theoretical basis for identifying and classifying the kinds of subjects a picture may have. She amplifies the first two modes by distinguishing between what a picture is *of* and what it is *about*. The *pre-iconographic level* consists of an objective (factual) description of the picture and a subjective (expressional) description. A factual description of a picture of woman and child, for example, would concentrate on the ordinary, recognizable, and everyday element in the picture, such as "woman and child." The expressional element can be the way the picture presents itself, what it conveys, e.g., "defeatist attitude". The *iconographic level* describes the cultural background of the picture. In order to identify that a man who raises his hat is greeting, one has to know of Western tradition and culture. Panofsky's two first levels can, according to Shatford (1986), be further subdivided corresponding to the following criteria: What does the picture represent (*Of*) and what does it express/is it about (*About*)? On the pre-iconographic level, *Of* covers the factual, whereas *About* refers to the expressional, i.e., an objective and subjective angle. On the iconographic level, *Of* may cover an objective view often expressed as a specific angle (for instance, a person mentioned by name), whereas *About* represents mythical or abstract contents. The above statements may be summarized by saying that each of Panofsky's first two levels contains two aspects expressed by *Of* and *About* (Ørnager, 1997).

Panofsky's three levels indicate a difference in presupposed knowledge, i.e., nothing (or only practical experience), special knowledge about image codes and literary sources, and special knowledge about the history of ideas, i.e., the culture. Barthes (1964; 1980) also employs levels in the reading of a picture. The first level does not demand any specific learning about image codes or other codes. To grasp this first level in the image we need only the knowledge attached to our perception or to use Panofsky's (1962) words "our familiarity with objects and events". To read the content of the image it is necessary to learn the semantic picture codes or, as Panofsky (1962) puts it, to have knowledge about image codes. According to Barthes (1961), that is closely attached to the culture from where the image is seen, and, according to Panofsky (1962), one needs to know about tradition and the history of ideas to be able to read the image. Although Panofsky bases his methodology on a study of Renaissance paintings and Barthes uses advertising photographs it is claimed that the two methodologies can be connected (Ørnager, 1997).

1.3   THE SHATFORD/PANOFSKY MATRIX

To analyze a photo more levels can be included, i.e., an *Of* or factual level and an *About* or expressional level where the latter is based on the cultural group utilizing the photo. The aspects should appear in the indexing of the picture as it is supposed to be of importance for the queries posed to a system containing photographs. Shatford's (Layne, 1994) levels are fine-tuned into four subject facets (who, what, where, and when) and it is suggested that each facet contains three aspects: specific of, generic of, and abstract. The matrix shown in Table 1.1 is often referred to as the Shatford/Panofsky model.

Table 1.1: Panofsky/Shatford classification matrix (Stewart, 2010)			
Shatford/ Panofsky	**Iconography Specifics = S**	**Pre-iconography Generics = G**	**Iconology Abstracts = A**
Who	Individually named person, group, thing (S1) Example: Obama, Eiffel tower, Sherlock Holmes, Jesus	Kind of person or thing G1 Example: woman, knight, tree, lion	Mythical or fictitious being A1 Example: Mother Earth, strength, hope, fear, Jesus (represented as a lamb)
What	Individually named event, action S2 Example: OL in London 2012	Kind of event, action, condition G2 Example: party, teach, dance, sleep, smile	Emotion or abstraction A2 Example: hopeful, creative
Where	Individually named geographical location S3 Example: Japan, Smithsonian National Zoo	Kind of place: geographical, architectural G3 Example: outdoors, botanical garden, road, kitchen	Place symbolized A3 Example: Hell, Heaven
When	Linear time: date or period S4 Example: June 2015	Cyclical time: season, time of day G4 Example: evening, spring, sunrise, Easter	Emotion, abstraction symbolized by time A4 Example: post-apocalypse, past, future

We do not want to grade the Panofsky/Shatford matrix but just point out that there are different interpretations of the levels in images (Christensen, 2017).

CHAPTER 2

Literature Review: State of the Art

In this chapter, we present a literary review and analysis of academic image research areas since the emergence of social media during the period of 2005–2017. Social media is primarily used as a new avenue for testing various hypothesizes. First, we describe three different methodologies, i.e., the Preferred Reporting Items for Systematic Reviews and Meta-Analyses guidelines (PRISMA) employed to locate the relevant literature. Second, a bibliometric analyzes visualizing co-citations of references and journals. Third, Grounded Theory is utilized to analyze the retrieved documents. After the presentation of the academic image, research papers are categorized and summarized.

2.1 PRISMA METHODOLOGY

The PRISMA (Moher et al., 2009) method is an evidence-based minimum set of items especially utilized within health care. However, it also can be employed as a basis for reporting reviews of other types of research. PRISMA focuses on ways in which authors can ensure a transparent and complete reporting of research and it is useful for critical evaluation purposes as well.

Based on an information science approach the following search terms are used in different combinations for the literary review: controlled vocabulary, crowdsourcing, image indexing, image retrieval, images, photo, photographic indexing, photographic retrieval, tags, subject access, subject headings, and visual information. The retrieved articles are then studied and 183 hits are left after removing duplicates. According to PRISMA, the records are screened for relevance where the criteria for inclusion are: (1) papers published between 2005 and 2017, both years included; (2) papers in English; and (3) peer-reviewed conference and journal articles. Exclusion criteria are: (1) papers with a predominantly technical description; and (2) papers focusing primarily on art paintings. The full text of the remaining 130 documents was reviewed for further evaluation according to the selection criteria. The assessment resulted in the inclusion of 71 papers in the review. The literature searches and selection process were completed by the authors (Figure 2.1).

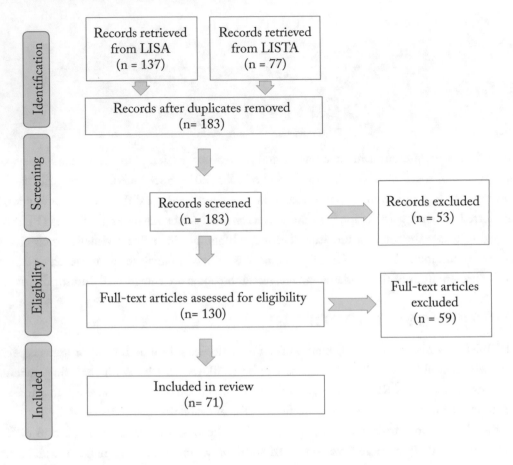

Figure 2.1: **PRISMA** chart of search strategy.

2.2   BIBLIOMETRIC NETWORKS BETWEEN THE ANALYZED DOCUMENTS

One way of gaining a visual overview of the relationship between analyzed documents is by means of bibliometric networks. In the research literature on bibliometric analysis, a multitude of bibliometric network visualizations has gained popularity.

According to Van Eck and Waltmann (2014), a bibliographic network can be characterized as a collection of nodes or entities and edges where a node is an object, such as an author or journal. The relationship between pairs of nodes denoted edge. According to Van Eck and Waltmann (2014) one of the most common uses of bibliometric network maps is co-citation networks. The co-citation networks are based on the citation of two publications simultaneously in a third publication. So, the idea is that the frequency with which two publication appears together as cited in a third publication is an expression of how strong the relationship is between the two co-cited publications. This idea was developed by Marshakov (1973) and Small (1973) and further investigated by Small and Griffith (1974). The co-citation concept was expanded and used to study relationships between researchers (White and Griffith, 1981) and relations between journals (McCain, 1991). According to Van Eck and Waltmann (2014), one classic example of co-citation network analysis is the study by White and McCain (1998) in which they study the researcher in the field of information science.

The assumption is that by analyzing the co-citation networks we can tell something about who is defining a domain either by looking at what works are co-cited or by looking at the individual researchers and their relationships to other researchers. An additionally important aspect is the relationship between domains and how one academic domain influences others. This also leads to the possibility of investigating how academic domains have developed chronologically.

In the literature study presented here, 72 research papers are included and cover approximately a 10-year span. To gain a better understanding of the development of the field of image indexing, two co-citation maps were generated from the Web of Knowledge citation database. Fifty-six of the 72 papers in the review were found indexed in Web of Knowledge and the full records including references were downloaded. The actual processing and generation of the co-citation maps were done using the VOS-viewer software version 1.6.5. VOS-viewer was developed by Van Eck and Waltmann from the University of Leiden in Belgium and it allows us to import Web of Knowledge data in a native format. Because of inconsistency in the Web of Knowledge data, corrections were made to author names and journal titles, securing a controlled list of authors and journal names. In some cases, changes in journal titles have occurred. In these cases, the current journal name has been used as a collative name. An example is the *Journal of the Association for Information Science and Technology* (*JASIST*) previously published under the title *Journal of the American Society for Information Science and Technology* and the *American Society for Information Science and Technology* (ASIST). In the downloaded records, all three names do appear.

In Figure 2.2, the co-citation map shows the ten papers with the most citations in the analyzed journal papers. The distance between the nodes appearing in the map is an indication of how "close" two papers can be considered to be. Papers appearing within a short distance of each other are often cited together.

The journal co-citation map in Figure 2.2 indicates two main clusters and identifies a central tendency focused around the journal (*JASIST*) and conference proceedings (ASIST) both published under the auspices of the Association of the Society for Information Science and Technology, previously known as the American Society for Information Science and Technology. Another dominant publication is *Information Processing and Management* (*IPM*) published by Elsevier. Given the focus in the reviewed papers this might not be surprising since all three publications can be considered core journals within the field of information science. The other journals in the co-citation map indicate an influence from other related fields to information science, mainly psychology and computer science. On the left side is *Cognitive Psychology* (Elsevier) with 29 citations and *Psychological Review* (American Psychological Association) with 10 citations. Computer science and related fields appear on the right side of the map, exemplified by *Lecture Notes in Computer Science*, receiving 34 citations, and a more specialized journal, *IEEE Transactions on Pattern Analysis and Machine Intelligence*.

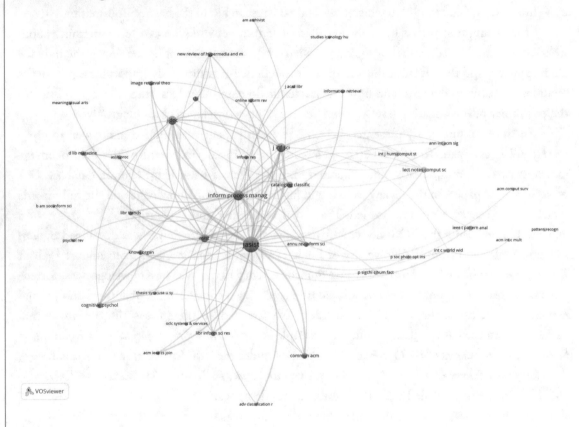

Figure 2.2: Co-citation map for cited journals.

Overall, the journal co-citation map indicates a strong center concentrated on information science but influenced both by the fields of psychology and computer science.

To get an overview of what research the reviewed papers build on, a co-citation analysis on cited papers were carried out. The resulting map (Figure 2.3) includes the 10 papers receiving the most citations, thus illustrating the research with the highest impact on the field of image indexing.

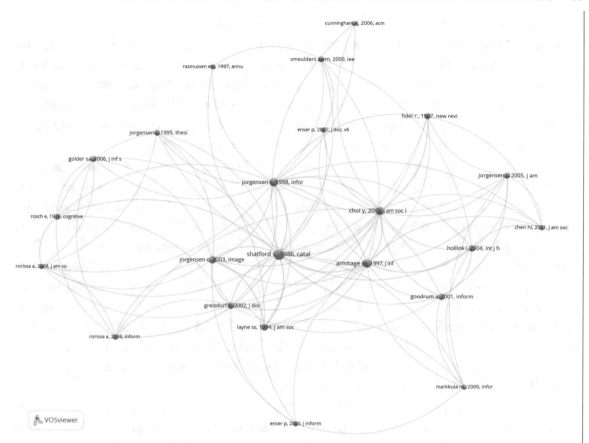

Figure 2.3: Co-citation map for cited references.

To get a view of the research papers cited by the reviewed papers, a co-citation map of the most cited papers was generated, in this case, papers with more than 10 citations in all 23 papers (Figure 2.3). The paper by Shatford (1986), where she presents her scheme for indexing images, had 26 references. In addition, Rorissa (2008) and Rorissa, Clough, and Deselars (2008) are often cited presenting his research on the indexing of photographs. Panofsky's interpretation model motivates Shatford in her 1986 article. Although Panofsky devises his theory for Renaissance art, Shatford utilizes his ideas for more concrete guidelines for indexing, stating that it is "possible to apply it to any representational work" (Shatford 1986, p. 43). Even though her article may seem dated and digitization has changed the environment, the Panofsky/Shatford model and the somewhat complicated constellation still have a strong impact on almost all research articles about the indexing of images. Rorissa acknowledges Shatford and her indexing proposals; however, as an academic influenced by social media Rorissa focuses on researchers, which are more suited for social networks. Rorissa looks to the area of psychology and cites Rosch et al.'s (1976) basic-level theory. Rorissa's goal is to find a categorization which can be easy handled by computers and nonprofessionals, and basic objects are the groupings that best mirror the correlational structure of the environment. Rorissa provides examples to support his research (see Figure 2.8) yet his ideas are not prominent in image indexing, perhaps because he is concerned with controlled index terms and sees tagging as additional uncontrolled information. The heritage of image indexing still guides the research areas although new methods conducted by professionals without the assistance of tagging and crowdsourcing seem to be so demanding of resources that practical implementation seems unlikely.

Jörgensen is represented with 4 papers where her 2003 paper receives 18 citations. The paper is about retrieval and suggests support for query modification. Most of Jörgensen's other writings are on the indexing of images and the development of coding schemes. In total, she is the most cited author, receiving 63 citations in all. Besides Jörgensen and Shatford (her 1994 paper on indexing is shown as Layne, S. S. in Figure 2.3), Rasmussen (1997) and Markkula and Sormunen (n.d.) are also cited for their work on image indexing. Only one of the cited papers is on collaborative tagging behavior: Golder and Huberman (2006). The paper by Golder is not on image indexing per se, but it is referred to by Shatford, Rouissa, and Rosch. The works of 4 authors are on aspects of information retrieval: Smeulders et al. (2000), Goodrum and Spink (2001), Enser (2000), and Fidel (1997). Two papers on user behavior and information search are cited: Armitage and Enser (1997) and Cunningham and Masoodian (2006). A few recent papers on image processing are referred to: Chen (2001) and Choi and Rasmussen (2003).

Fifteen of the papers are published from 2000 and onward, 6 papers are published between 1990 and 1999, and 2 papers before 1990. This is in line with other citation patterns where the bulk of the cited papers are within a relatively short chronological span from the publication year of the citing papers; however, analysis also illustrates that central papers for the domain receive citations long after publication, as Shatford (1986) shows.

2.3   ANALYZING THE RESEARCH PAPERS WITH GROUNDED THEORY

Grounded Theory is selected for further examination. Grounded Theory is a qualitative method developed by Glaser and Strauss (1967) and operationalized by Strauss and Corbin (1990; 1998) and Glaser (1992). Its techniques for data collection and analysis are designed to allow concepts and categories to emerge from the data. Grounded Theory works with codes (core categories), categories, and properties. The development of categories is based on observations, interviews, and questionnaires as well as on existing literature. Grounded Theory is simply the discovery of emerging patterns in data (Walsh et al., 2015).

Definitions are offered by Strauss and Corbin (1990, p. 61). They define *Code* as, "*Conceptual labels placed on discrete happenings, events, and other instances of phenomena*"; *Category* as, "*A classi-*

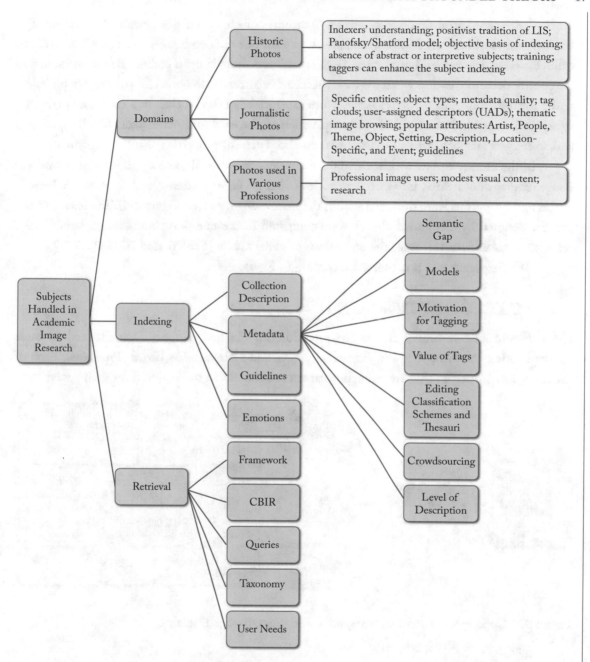

Figure 2.4: Code, categories, and sub-categories deduced by Grounded Theory where Metadata has sub-sub-categories and Domain has properties.

fication of concepts", and finally *Property* as, "Attributes or characteristics pertained to a category". Strauss and Corbin's definitions, which are chosen for our data on images, are related to what we call: classes, categories, and properties. Data is analyzed first via open coding. Based on induction we specify occurrences and when we have sufficient occurrences to observe a pattern, we provide a name for the group, i.e., a *category name*. More categories can form a class or a code. The main category outlines a kind of empirical road map, which can be used for further data collection, sorting, and to suggest sub-categories. Occurrences can also represent properties of sub-categories.

In the literary review we identified the main category, the code, as *Subjects handled in academic image research* and divided into three categories called *Domains*, *Indexing*, and *Retrieval*. Sub-categories and properties were deducted within the main categories (see Figure 2.4). The results of the process denoted by Grounded Theory were compared to the question about "… academic image research areas undertaken since the emergence of social media in the period 2005–2017."

The following text is organized according to Figure 2.4.

2.4   CATEGORY DOMAINS

Using Figure 2.5, we briefly explain the procedure for the first category Domains and its three sub-categories, i.e., *Historic photos*, *Journalistic photos*, and *Photos used in Various Professions*. Each of the latter has properties that are indications about the content in the analyzed research papers.

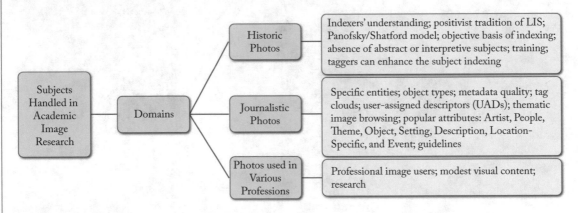

Figure 2.5: Code, category, and sub-categories with properties for Domains.

2.4.1   HISTORIC PHOTOS

Since Springer et al. (2008) issued the report on "The Library of Congress' Flickr Pilot Project," where non-professionals included supplementary tags to already indexed historical photos, there has been much interest about indexing ancient photos. Stewart (2010) accomplishes an exploratory study of current indexing practices. The research uses a qualitative methodology to explore the particular phenomenon of indexing as a human activity system situated in the social environment of organizations. The positivist tradition of Library and Information Science (LIS) clearly demonstrates the overwhelming use of subject headings related to specific or generic things using the Panofsky/Shatford model (see Table 1.1). The absence of abstract or interpretive subjects suggests that there is a fundamental gap in the access to the subject content of historic photographs. Stewart (2010) suggests that an improved understanding of the current library indexing, its strengths and limitations, may help institutions holding historic photograph collections to evaluate how well this type of indexing meets the needs of their user groups. Stewart (2015) continues his examination of historical images but this time he divides his study into two parts. The first part involves 10 professional indexers and 28 Flickr photos. Panofsky/Shatford's model is again utilized for indexing in the 2015 study, although the findings demonstrate that indexers do not view subjects in the same way as described in Panofsky/Shatford's matrix. The indexers focus on factual indexing of both generic and specific subjects and almost completely avoid abstract terms. The findings also point to an approach to indexing historical photographs based on a traditional paradigm. A problem seems to be that professional indexers don't provide a great range of intellectual subject indexing. The second part involves 66 students without training and 33 Flickr photos of which 22 have some metadata. The Panofsky/Shatford model is again applied. Tags for untitled and titled photographs indicate that accompanied metadata had little influence on the tags. In a second stage, 28 students of the 66 were trained to measure whether this intervention had any significance. A key difference was that the trained participants contributed twice as many tags as the baseline group. The general findings show that students prefer generic tags, with specific and abstract tags used almost equally. Taggers are interested in more than the pre-iconographic subject matter that indexers focus on. The results from the second stage demonstrate that a training intervention has a significant effect on increasing the numbers of tags. The different approaches by indexers and students offer the possibility that taggers can enhance the subject indexing provided by professional indexers by being more specific.

Why are photographs interesting?

Louise Broch

Photographs are very interesting because they provide the opportunity to glare at the picture continuously. I never stop looking at still photographs and I always experience new details. When you work with videos, you are not able to appreciate the details unless you stop the film. The still photograph can capture a moment in time, something you never experience with video.

Photographs are part of our cultural heritage and through them we meet users. The Danish Broadcasting Corporation (DR) unleashed 77,000 press photographs last year, and involved our users in tagging them by crowdsourcing. In half a year we have around 100,000 tags on these photographs. Now the collection is open to the public and utilized to hunt for images about cultural heritage. The DR journalists employ the tags as well and claim that for them retrieval of press photographs is more controlled.

Louise Broch is an Information Specialist at the Danish Broadcasting Corporation's (DR) Archive and Process. She holds a master's degree in Digital Journalism and one in Music. She has more than 15 years of experience with research and archiving at DR. In 2014, DR Archive formed a team with the objective of focusing on public outreach in new, creative ways with archival material to meet DR's audience wherever they are situated. Louise is the manager of this group.

The first sub-category, *Historic Photos*, has the properties (see Figure 2.5): indexers' understanding, positivist tradition of LIS, Panofsky/Shatford model, objective basis of indexing, absence of abstract or interpretive subjects, training, taggers can enhance the subject indexing. It communicates that we face indexing principles based on positivist traditions utilizing a model developed by Panofsky/Shatford. Furthermore, the positivist approach is objective and the trained indexer must not make any personal interpretation of historic photos (Lancaster, 2003). Tagging done by taggers can be a supplement to the indexing (done by professionals), however, taggers must be trained, enabling them to focus on the semantic pitfalls (Stewart, 2010; 2015). What the data suggests is that taggers can help the specialists but training is required. An answer to the research question is that there is no major change in the endorsed research after social media appeared. However, professionals value the assistance from taggers. Any spillover as to how to manage historical images on social media is not noticeable.

2.4.2   JOURNALISTIC PHOTOGRAPHS

Westman and Oittinen (2006) published an article based on a Finnish experiment among photo journalists. Interviews and observations of nine staff members (three archivists, one journalist, one editor, one graphic artist, two image journalists, and one photographer) were conducted and log analyses were completed of 1,852 queries from the image search logs of the editorial system in a daily Finnish newspaper. Their results indicate that most image queries and requests deal with specific entities, but that object types are also common. Thematic image needs seem fulfilled by end-user searching and browsing. Image retrieval tasks are highly influenced by contextual factors. Two years later, Neal (2008) studied different job groups, i.e., photojournalists and news librarians' preference for image metadata within an online photograph archival system, and photographs without restrictions imposed on their descriptions. She tested 102 participants from various online photo discussion lists by qualitative and quantitative questions, including 11 image retrieval methods:

Burford, Briggs, and Eakins's (2003) model, consisting of nine categories of information that may be associated with an image; browsing; and user-assigned descriptors (UADs). All job groups favor metadata about Named Objects, Specific Events, Browsing, UADs, and Size/Date/Photographer. However, they have concerns about the metadata quality present in their captions and keywords. Based on their responses, authoritative, subject-based representation methods, such as Thesaurus for Graphic Materials (TGM) or Library of Congress Subject Headings (LCSH), simply were not used in the news environments included in this study, neither by photojournalism professionals nor by news librarians. Hence, some news photo departments have implemented local solutions to these problems. Neal suggested new approaches to facilitate a search of news photographs, e.g., integration of tag clouds into the user interface of photograph archival systems which may help guide users to the correct spellings of common keywords. Chen et al. (2010) examined the archive site of Pictures of the Year International (POYi), which is a renowned annual photo-journalism contest that began in 1943. The image collection and contest managed by POYi is a program of the Donald W. Reynolds Journalism Institute at the University of Missouri, School of Journalism. End users' search terms were analyzed using Jörgensen's 12 categories (Jörgensen, 1995). The study identified eight of the most popular attributes (a total of 87.94%), i.e., Artist, People, Theme, Object, Setting, Description, Location-Specific, and Event. These attributes may guide potential users in providing meaningful tags to the POYi images, so it may be worthwhile to suggest to visitors to use some/all of the above attributes to tag images.

The second sub-category, *Journalistic Photos,* has the properties (see Figure 2.5): specific entities, object types, metadata quality, tag clouds, UADs, thematic image browsing, popular attributes: artist, people, theme, object, setting, description, location-specific, event, and guidelines. Journalists normally own their photos. It was learned that handling journalistic photos is about how different organizations/media (newspapers, broadcasting, journalistic institutes, stock photos, etc.) categorize the photos. In general, indexing demonstrates a division between specific entities and objects types where the first represents persons in a photo and the latter points to different motives, where the persons are not the main subject. The various journalistic media also have individual classifications based on attributes in the photo, and when it comes to retrieval the suggestion is to browse by separate attributes (Neal, 2008). Accordingly, guidelines are presented as positive and essential especially for new employees (Westman and Oittinen, 2006; Chen et al., 2010). There is little change in the research about journalistic photos. There was a suggestion, after the appearance of social media, to have UADs in indexing and to utilize tag clouds in retrieval (Neal, 2008).

2.4.3 PHOTOS USED IN VARIOUS PROFESSIONS

Beaudoin (2014) studied how and why a group of 20 archaeologists, architects, art historians, and artists use images. She utilized qualitative research methods where surveys and semi-structured interviews are the main components. She discovered that archaeologists and art historians use images within their lecture presentations for research and publication. Architects and artists mostly use images for research and design creation. Her conclusion was that the library and information science community has only recently begun to address visual information and research to date has failed to adequately address image users' needs regarding how and why images are used.

The last sub-category, *Photos Used in Various Professions,* has the properties (see Figure 2.5): professional image users, modest visual content, and research. The professionals (from different areas) have different ways of employing images. The sub-category shows new trends in academic image research as it focuses on the useof images in different domains (Beaudoin, 2014). Within the domain the visual content is used very modestly. It may be a research area for different professions to look into. In general, the knowledge about managing photos is not equally important for all domains. There is no major change in the endorsed research after the appearance of social media.

Table 2.1: Category Domains with sub-categories		Publication Per Year
Domain: Historic Photos	2010: Stewart	1
	2015: Stewart	1
Domain: Journalistic Photos	2006: Westman and Oittinen	1
	2008: Neal	1
	2010: Chen et al.	1
Domain: Other Areas	2014: Beudoin	1

The general findings show that students prefer generic tags, with specific and abstract tags used almost equally. Taggers are interested in more than the pre-iconographic subject matter that academic indexers focus on. A few results demonstrate that a training intervention has a significant effect in increasing the number of tags. Attributes can guide potential users in providing meaningful tags to the images, so it may be worthwhile to suggest that users apply specific attributes when tagging images. Categorization of and searching among attributes in photos (AOIs), together with utilization of tag clouds and development of a brief training, are helpful suggestions that may be adopted by various groups within social networks. However, although different approaches by academic indexers and students may suggest that taggers can enhance the subject indexing by being more specific, the results are for professional indexing and not for organizing personal photos on social media.

2.5   CATEGORY INDEXING

In the category *Indexing* we have four sub-categories (see Figure 2.6) with different representations. The first three—*Collection description*, *Metadata*, and *Guidelines*—contain papers at the general level, studying collections and the way these are indexed. The last one, *Emotions,* handles papers on specific issues. All authors mentioned under the sub-categories are shown in Table 2.11 at the end of this chapter.

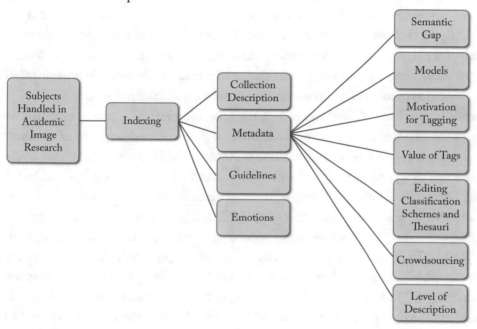

Figure 2.6: Code, category, and sub-categories for Indexing where Metadata has sub-sub-categories.

2.5.1   COLLECTION DESCRIPTION

Collection Description is represented by only one paper (Harkema and Avery, 2015) mostly concerned with practical considerations around handling photos in a specific database: The Canadian Courtney Milne's Collection at the University of Saskatchewan archives. The authors published an article about how the format of the work influences issues surrounding reproduction rights, access, and use in unexpected ways. Facets of collection development like access, use, and marketability are issues common to many contemporary image collections. Harkema and Avery shed light on some of the problems, as they were able to develop solutions for especially technical challenges in the Milne project. Most professionals may be very interested in this practical approach. However, new or different research strategies are absent for handling professional photos and there is no spillover to social media. The authors suggest development and management of a database. Access, use, and marketability, however, may well be useful for social media as there are commercial interests involved in this medium.

2.5.2   METADATA

The second sub-category, *Metadata,* is roughly concerned with different kinds of data describing images. Numerous controlled approaches, like classification schemes and thesauri, are employed, and, additionally, papers deal with un-controlled issues like crowdsourcing and tagging. The controlled methodologies concern levels of description, including the question about *Aboutness,* standards for descriptions of images, semantic gap, and design of metadata schemes. The un-controlled is about user-organized systems, access and connectivity, taxonomy of motivation, etc.

Enser, Sandom, and Lewis (2005) focused on the semantic gap, which can be explained as the difference between a human description of visual media and a machine description of the same. They studied the integration of Content-Based Image Retrieval (CBIR) techniques with traditional textual metadata as a possible means of achieving "semantic" image retrieval. They utilized a test collection of 14 organizations' digital images. The conclusion in 2005 was that the richness of the manual annotations clearly indicates the necessity of enhancing the functionality of current automatic annotation techniques, if there is to be any possibility of the semantic gap connecting with real-world applications. To credit future CBIR research they also suggest developing an appropriate ontology, which describes the relationships between the labels and concepts with which they are associated. Jörgensen (2007) concentrates again on the semantic gap and additional social tagging in image access. With the development of automated methods of CBIR, the term *semantic gap* to Jörgensen has come to refer to the larger issue of the gap between these image low-level features, and the context-sensitive meanings humans associate with these. Her understanding is much the same as the one expressed by Enser et al. (2005). Although the controlled vocabulary paradigm that the only "good" tag is a controlled tag is seen as the basis of most studies, her question is: Why should users trade a process that allows spontaneity and even fun for one which requires effort and seriousness, not to mention learning? In other words, Jörgensen foresees that new paradigms are taking shape. The act of tagging embodies the concepts of interactivity, connectivity, and access, which are characteristics of the digital age and which presume the user to be capable and seeking connection. Although Jörgensen indicates a change in image categorization, there is no major change in her research after the introduction of social media.

Table 2.2: Category Indexing with sub-category Metadata and semantic gap

		Publication Per Year
Indexing—Metadata— Semantic Gap	2005: Enser, Sandom, and Lewis	1
	2007: Jörgensen	1

Models are frequently studied within academic image research, and Rafferty and Hidderley (2007) examine three models of subject indexing (i.e., expert-led, author-generated, and user-orientated) and two user-orientated indexing approaches, Flickr and the Democratic Indexing project, which are examples of systems that offer alternatives to imposed semantic structures. Both systems were initially developed to offer approaches to image retrieval. It might be that the indexing practice is not an activity that demands either author-based indexing or user-based indexing, but rather that options regarding *Knowledge Organization* tools and methods depending on the format and content of the signs (text-based symbolic signs or indexical and iconological images), and the function of the retrieval activity. They focus on a blended indexing approach, which seems the most promising when deciding on image management.

A couple of years later, Stvilia and Jörgensen (2009) identified ten categories of characteristics that Flickr users might use for forming digital photo collections. The study contributes to a better understanding of user-generated collections and the need in these collections for various types of collection-level metadata. The results recommend more research into the design of metadata schemas and assistance to improve organization and access to images in both traditional databases and emerging social contexts of image description and use. Although the paper does not provide an exact model for image indexing, it points to the most promising candidates (10 characteristics) for un-controlled indexing.

Angus, Stuart, and Thelwall (2010) presented another indexing model where they explore academic terms used for tagging photos in Flickr, and examine how they differ between subject areas. No research in 2010 focuses on visual typologies for Flickr images. This is an important gap to fill because knowing what kind of images people upload gives insight into how and why Flickr is useful. Angus et al. used 12 academic subject categories on Flickr from the Arts and Humanities Citation Index (AHCI), the Science Citation Index (SCI), and the Social Science Citation Index (SSCI). The paper concentrates on general pictorial analysis of images (i.e., whether the image is of a person, a sunset, a building, etc.) and the secondary iconographic level of analysis (which requires an interpretation of the objects in the picture based on a certain level of familiarity with the cultural context), and follows content analysis methodology approaches. The authors suggest that the model can be used as a marketing tool to show case images of an institution, as a way for existing students to share images, and as a way for specific departments/academics to be able to re-enter information and images from specific events (e.g., conferences, symposia, workshops, etc.). The results of this research illustrate that Flickr can be useful to academics as an image resource. It can serve as a database in which subject-relevant images can be searched for in whatever way necessary, although this may depend on subject area and the reasons behind the use of the system. Beaudoin (2012) presented a framework as a result of an analysis of digital content. She finds that the primary topics addressed in the digital preservation literature are the ones that focus on technological and semantic information. The paper surveys various discussions in the literature surrounding contextual information. Her framework explicitly manages the various dimensions of context of which eight distinct dimensions are useful for digital preservation. Each dimension has multiple characteristics that she suggests be further developed. Although her framework is not an exact model, it presents a search for providing prototypes for indexing (controlled and un-controlled) in the digital era.

Fauzi and Belkhatir (2013) observe that many earlier discussed classification methodologies conform to Panofsky's theory. They propose a classification framework along the same line for classifying image contextual information into five facets: signal, object, scene, abstract, and relational. The classification framework is in accordance with Panofsky's theory, where there are generic (pre-iconographic) and specific (iconographic) image entities under the *object* facet. Their *abstract* facet corresponds to the iconologic class. Regretfully, detailed information about the user study is not provided. The proposed model takes a web page, extracts all images and the contextual information, converts it into a set of indexing terms, and then, for each term, classifies it into one or more of the five semantic facets. Natural Language Processing (NLP) techniques and a knowledge resource (WordNet) are used for the classification. The classification is performed automatically with the raw image contextual information extracted from any general web page and is not solely based on image tags. Furthermore, the syntactical relationships (from a linguistic analysis) between faceted terms are leveraged to construct the multifaceted indexes. Fauzi and Belkhatir (2014) continued the study of web image indexing and retrieval frameworks. They provided the anatomy of a generic context-based web image understanding framework and proposed its stage-based breakdown, covering topical issues from information indexing and retrieval, image description models, etc. They reviewed state-of-the-art solutions in the literature categorized and analyzed in light of the techniques used. An image descriptor model of the five facets from the 2013 study is considered. The generic and specific descriptors, which are broad in essence, should be used in conjunction with a first step of classification into one of the proposed facets.

Table 2.3: Category Indexing with sub-category Metadata and Models		
		Publication Per Year
Indexing—Metadata—Models	2007: Rafferty and Hidderley	1
	2009: Stvilia and Jörgensen	1
	2010: Angus, Stuart, and Thelwall	1
	2012: Beaudoin	1
	2013: Fauzi and Belkhatir	1
	2014: Fauzi and Belkhatir	1

Ames and Naaman (2007) examined motivation for tagging images on Flickr and ZoneTag via qualitative methods. They interviewed 13 participants who have taken the most photos on social media. They studied the possibility to motivate users to annotate content, and it appears that point-of-capture annotation (e.g., on the mobile device) can encourage the addition of tags. Tag suggestions and other methods of assisting mobile annotation proved to have broad implications. The study shows that organization for oneself is a more common motivation than communication for oneself, while communication with friends and family is a more common motivation than organization for friends and family, and that organization for the public is a much more common motivation than communication. It appears that the motivations for adding contextual tags, which tended to be very personal, are largely unrelated to the motivations for adding tags for the public, namely, to make one's photos findable and to gain reputation in the Flickr community. The motivation is personal communication with friends and family while the tags are more organizational for the public.

Nov and Ye (2010) studied tagging motivation on Flickr. The authors utilized the study summarized above to look at the difference between the function of organization and the function of communication. They studied these functions in categories of intended audience of the tags: self, friends, and family, and the public of Flickr users. For the test, they involved 251 Flickr users who had at least 1 publicly viewable photo. The findings of the survey suggest that both social presence and individual level motivations affect users' tagging level, with the exception of the family and friends motivation. The social-presence drivers seem to be stronger predictors of users' tagging, which comes as no surprise given the collaborative, public nature of websites such as Flickr. The number of photos a user has is also a predictor of tagging level, as expected. Social presence proved to have a positive effect on tagging in the present study, and suggests that developers of content-sharing systems focus efforts in this area by showing users the benefits of contacts. Although this study concerns only Flickr photos it clearly demonstrates the advantage of supporting the users with added contacts via social media. Petek (2012) manages a study in which tagging motivation is one issue, and where she analyzes the difference between librarians and users in creating metadata on images. She utilized ten images in total, i.e., five from Flickr tagged by Flickr visitors and five from Digital Library of Slovenia (dLib.si) indexed by librarians. Eighty students participated in the test from the Department of Library and Information Science and Book Studies of the Faculty of Arts, University of Ljubljana. The number of assigned tags for the ten photos differed greatly among participants, librarians, and Flickr visitors where participants are the heaviest taggers. The cognitive aspect of categorization is evident, ranging from general to specific tags. The results show that for two-thirds of the students the motivation is personal benefit while one-third of tags are for community benefit. This last study shows the same trend as the other papers when focusing on motivation for tagging, i.e., personal benefit. The motivation papers do not check previous assumptions but study new research questions. Social networks are the focus of research.

Drew and Guillemin (2014) introduced an "interpretive engagement" framework to comprise three stages of meaning-making: through participant engagement, through research-driven engagement, and through re-contextualizing. Each of these phases is limited but in combination provide rich and comprehensive visual analysis. To test the statement, participants aged 10–19 years were presented with a throwaway camera. The tests ask the participants to create a series of photographs to show what it was like to live with an ongoing health condition, and what actions they might complete to take care of their health. This analytic framework is predominantly researcher-driven with an emphasis on close inspection and engaging with the details of each image. Researchers are accustomed to working within appropriate ethical parameters with written texts, however, visual images add another layer of complexity, in particular, when identifying material is included or multiple interpretations of abstract images are possible. To ensure that visual research methodologies are gaining acceptance and are legitimate there is a need for sound analytic processes. Drew and Guillemin (2014) proposed the interpretive engagement framework as a rigorous and systematic analytic method for participant-generated visual images. The implementation of this interpretive framework offers the potential for rich and thorough interpretations and analysis.

Table 2.4: Category Indexing with sub-category Metadata and Motivation for Tagging		
		Publication Per Year
Indexing—Metadata— Motivation for Tagging	2007: Ames and Naaman	1
	2010: Oden Nov and Chen Ye	1
	2012: Petek	1
	2014: Drew and Guillemin	1

Ransom and Raferty (2011) examined the value of tags by looking at whether the way users tag images is similar to the way they search for images. Specifically, the study considers if image tags describe the same properties or facets of an image as those that are present/utilized in image queries. They tested Flickr images by using Shatford's matrix and 2,000 tags from 250 images.

The results confirm earlier research into image tagging, which shows that generic terms are more common in image descriptions than specific terms, and that abstract terms are rarely used. When comparing image tags with query terms, the results of this research show that there are clear similarities in the facets that are present in tags and in query terms, with terms relating to people and objects, or locations, being the most commonly used in both cases. This can suggest that the aspects of images that users include in their image tags are the same as those that are of interest to users in their searches.

Huang and Jörgensen (2013) studied whether popular tags in Flickr change over time, if there are differences in tagging non-domain and domain areas, and if metadata has any influence on tagging in both Flickr and the Library of Congress's photo-stream (LCP) on Flickr. They examined all the questions by comparing the popular tag frequency rankings and tag categories in the entire Flickr General Collection (FGC) during the years 2006 and 2010, respectively. About 140 tags from FGC and from LCP on Flickr were studied. Those popular tags related to generic objects and events show a high metadata usage ratio, while those related to specific locations and objects showed a low ratio. Popular tags reflect the culture of the tagging population and serve as evidence of the social impact of collaborative social-tagging activities. The same year Jörgensen, Stvilia, and Wu (2013) examined the terms users assign to images as tags, and the terms users choose to create a query for an image, and whether these were the same terms. They tested ten historical photographs in the LCP on Flickr. In the first phase, the participants are 35 students and staff members, and in the second phase 25 students and staff members from the College of Communication and Information at Florida State University (same group as in Stvilia, Jörgensen, and Wu, 2012). Results from the coding reveal that, for the queries, the Objects and Story Classes account for the greatest percent of the query terms, with People and People-Related Attributes following close behind. The findings of this study indicate that several quality criteria of image indexing are different from those of textual document indexing, such as context, moods, importance, and level of detail. The fact that image content is not linguistic, and that the process requires translating sensory input into socially defined and culturally justified linguistic labels and identifiers, can explain the differences in the quality of criteria of image indexing.

Terras (2011) studied the growing trend of the creation of digital images of cultural and heritage materials beyond library, art gallery, or museum walls, with a particular focus on the use of the image-hosting site Flickr. The paper is somewhat similar to the tagging of historic images reported by Springer et al. (2008), however, Terras is not only focusing on tags but on amateurs hosting, discussing, and collecting image information in certain fields. In her tryouts, she interviewed ten frequent users of Flickr, and identified five well-used and well-populated pools/groups. Digitization by amateurs, a phenomenon previously ignored by information professionals, is providing a rich source of online cultural heritage content that often documents areas not covered by traditional institutions. Therefore, the most successful examples of this approach can teach best practices to traditional memory institutions about how to make their collections useful, interesting, and used by online communities. Linking stand-alone institutional websites into websites such as Flickr, which have a built-in audience, and encouraging the public to contribute relevant material to institutional digital collections may provide a way to increase the use of digitized heritage content. Kovács and Takács (2014) asked if it was possible to conduct an effective natural language search in library image collections. They approached the question in three steps. First, they examined the metadata, second, the data structure, and third, formulas required for the search. They used a modified version of the Dublin Core (ISO, 2009), a relational data model, and functions of a search system used for sorting image documents based on their information. These functions are based on a mathematical model of communication, which in turn is based on research by Norbert Wiener (1948) and Claude E. Shannon (1948). During searches, they introduced a new concept: informativity defined as the amount of information, on average, carried by one element (keyword) of the image. They claimed that in an image there is altogether one dominant image element, which has a higher score. They concluded that it is possible to conduct a new and effective natural language search in the image collections of digital libraries. This paper is managed under the category *Indexing* although it also concerns *Retrieval*. As noted before, it is a choice whether to consider the paper as related to indexing or retrieval, as they are complimentary issues.

Table 2.5: Category Indexing with sub-category Metadata and Value of Tags		
		Publication Per Year
Indexing—Metadata—Value of Tags	2011: Ransom and Raferty;	1
	Terras	1
	2013: Huang and Jörgensen;	1
	Jöorgensen, Stvila, and Wu	1
	2014: Kovács and Takács	1

Yoon (2009) explored editing classification schemes and thesauri when she studied user-supplied tags and how they are applied to designing a thesaurus that reflects the unique features of image documents. Shatford's facet category (1986; Layne, 1994) and Rosch et al.'s (1976) basic-level theory examine concepts to be included in a thesaurus. The study demonstrates how user-supplied tags successfully can select concepts to be included in a thesaurus and in identifying semantic relations among those selected concepts. The results suggest that the best approach, especially for Color and Generic category descriptors, is to focus on basic-level terms and to include frequently used superordinate- and subordinate-level terms (see Figure 2.8). The results also indicate a need for greater inclusion of levels, here especially specific category terms, which are shown to be an important tool in establishing related tags. Color is mentioned in the result, which is a bit strange as color is one of the pieces of "factual information" catered to by CBIR, and information has been tested since 1999 by IBM (Rui, Huang, and Chang, 1999). Apart from this, it seems a good idea to have user involvement in providing additional tags when editing a thesaurus.

Stvillia and Jörgensen (2010) reported about the results of an exploratory study of Flickr member activities around photographs from the Library of Congress photo-stream on Flickr. The tags from the photo-stream related to two *Knowledge Organization* systems: the Thesaurus for Graphic Materials (TGM) and the Library of Congress Subject Headings (LCSH). The study suggests that these tags can complement traditional methods of indexing using controlled vocabularies. Stvilia, Jörgensen, and Wu (2012) continued to look at user involvement in indexing. They studied the social terms from Flickr and the English Wikipedia and examined whether they have the potential to add value to the TGM and the LCSH by providing additional access points. Ten photos from LC Flickr photo-stream are used for a test. In the first phase, 35 students and staff members participated and in the second phase 25 students and staff members were recruited from the College of Communication and Information at Florida State University. The experiments, using various algorithms, confirm that the social terms did add value relative to terms from the controlled vocabularies. The median rating for the usefulness of social terms was significantly higher than the baseline rating, but was lower than the ratings for the terms from the TGM and the LCSH. Complementing the controlled vocabulary terms with social terms more than doubled the average coverage of participants' terms for a photograph. Participants with more tagging and indexing experience assigned a greater number of tags than did other participants. There is no doubt about the positive effect of user involvement in indexing cited by the papers. The last conclusion that participants with indexing experience assign more tags contradicts Petek's (2012) study, which presented the opposite statement, however, this can be because "people with indexing experience" are not considered librarians.

Benson (2015) provided an overview of the relationship problem as described in the LIS literature. The focus of the review is on semantic relationships presented in the descriptions of photographs applied to visual information and linguistic representations. He proposed two modes of description as a framework for guiding and limiting this discussion about the literature: machine-readable description and phenomenal description. Many studies focus on indexing image attributes and analysis of image search logs measuring user behavior. Recognition and analysis of relationships among objects and their properties, for the most part, remains an elusive subject. A significant amount of time and labor has already gone into building image-indexing systems used in large-scale enterprises. Two of the better-known controlled vocabularies are the TGM and the Art and Architecture Thesaurus (AAT). Among the problems of representing these systems in structures that represent knowledge are limitations on the number and types of relationships allowed in controlled vocabularies and problems minimizing ambiguity.

Table 2.6: Category Indexing with sub-category Metadata and Editing Classification Schemes and Thesauri

		Publication Per Year
Indexing—Metadata— Editing Classification Schemes and Thesauri	2009: Yoon	1
	2010: Stvillia and Jörgensen	1
	2012: Stvillia, Jörgensen, and Wu	1
	2015: Benson	1

Crowdsourcing—the wisdom of the crowd—is analyzed by the Spanish researchers Estellés-Arolas and González-Ladrón-de-Guevara (2012). They present papers that define crowdsourcing. Their research defines common elements of crowdsourcing and establishes the basic characteristics of any crowdsourcing initiative. Although the term "crowdsourcing" is constantly evolving, it can be defined as a type of participative online activity where a group of individuals voluntarily undertakes a task. The undertaking of the task always entails mutual benefit. Through the analysis of all the definitions, eight characteristics common to any given crowdsourcing initiative were found. The authors then provided a wide definition that covers the majority (if not all) of existing crowdsourcing processes.

Nakatsu, Grossman, and Iacovou (2014) also conducted an extensive study of crowdsourcing. Their goal was to provide a framework for better understanding of the approaches, and to classify them in terms of the types of tasks for which they are best suited. The framework for development of the taxonomy on crowdsourcing derives from the literature on task complexity and the study of virtual teams. The perspective is that, carefully managed and fit to the right task, crowdsourcing can be a powerful tool to solve a wide range of problems. As interest in crowdsourcing approaches continues to grow, it becomes essential to understand the breadth and depth of options available. Although many are aware of crowdsourcing there is a lack of understanding of how to use it most effectively. Lin et al. (2015) studied 1,986 representative images from the Teenie Harris (photo) Archive, an image collection from the Carnegie Museum of Art. Their aim was to learn about the crowdsourcing of photos indexed with and without descriptions, and to check whether the provision of descriptions influences users in their tagging behavior. They tested 1,986 representative images with a first group of 97 participants without any image description. The second group of 159 participants was able to see image descriptions. The results of the analysis demonstrated that tags produced without image descriptions have a much smaller overlap with the words used in description than the tags produced when the description was displayed to taggers. However, none of the conditions is better than the other in a practical sense. When indexers produce image tags without text description they tend to use more generic terms that increase tag density and make images more findable. The data suggest that a mix of tags produced with and without any description could be more helpful for image search than one of these conditions alone. Social networks are not the focus of studying crowdsourcing. Technology is involved in managing more people but handled outside the social networks.

Table 2.7: Category Indexing with sub-category Metadata and Crowdsourcing

		Publication Per Year
Indexing—Metadata—Crowd-sourcing	2012: Estellés-Arolas and González-Ladrón-de-Guevara	1
	2014: Nakatsu, Grossman, and Iacovou	1
	2015: Lin et al.	1

"Level of Description" was a study by Klenczon and Rygiel (2014) where they researched the level, to be adapted for images, and the indexing tool(s) for successful use. Low-level properties of an image, such as shape, texture, and color, contribute to the understanding of an image, but do not define it, and text-based search techniques remain the most efficient and accurate methods for image retrieval. The authors analyzed several standards and practices of some large libraries and museums. *The Cataloging Cultural Objects: A Guide to Describing Cultural Works and Their Images* (CCO) (Baca et al., 2006; Harpring, 2009) is, according to Klenczon and Rygiel (2014), the most complex and popular among data content standards. When indexing images Klenczon and Rygiel (2014) exploit JHP BN (National Library of Poland Subject Headings) controlled vocabulary as subject terms, genre/form terms, or keywords, recorded in several MARC 21 fields. They use the Panofsky/Shatford model, aiming to enumerate general and secondary elements of a picture; however, images may be perceived without language barriers and it is essential to provide multilingual access points as descriptive metadata.

The same year, Rafferty and Albinfalah (2014) evaluated the potential to draw on users' interpretations of images in the design of a model for a story-based image indexing system. Their concern was with the input side of the user-based indexing process. The project took a first step toward exploring the potential of using narratives to design a story-based image indexing system. They tested two images with 26 MSc distance learner students from Aberystwyth University and used qualitative research methods involving semi-structured interviews. Overall, the results of the interview stage indicated the existence of story elements in the participants' descriptions. Data analysis allowed for the development of relevant categories, such as "setting", "character", and "plot" to understand the construction of the narratives. The goal for many scholars has been to design image retrieval systems, which can capture meaning and develop indexing approaches at pre-iconographic, iconographic, and iconological levels (Panofsky, 1939). Differences in interpretation are likely to come at the connotative level (see Figure 1.1), and at this level, storytelling might offer a particularly rich input method, as it appears to encourage creative and more varied responses. It might be that the ubiquitous form of the story would allow the development of a relatively structured but intuitive method of inputting interpretative content. If storytelling develops as a method of indexing, it might be that analytical algorithms based on the conventions of the story can identify and process story elements as individual terms. Zeng, Graces, and Žumer (2014) suggested an automatic semantic analysis tool called Open Calais. They created subject access points by utilizing Panofsky's three-layer theory (Panofsky, 1939) that is the basis for subject analysis of all cultural objects, as suggested by the content standard CCO (Baca et al., 2006; Harpring, 2009). Simplified by CCO, the three layers become: (1) description (referring to the generic elements); (2) identification (referring to the specific subject); and (3) interpretation (referring to the meaning or themes represented by the subjects). The analysis results in dozens and, at times, hundreds of potential entities and social tags. The conclusion is that entities and tags correspond almost exclusively to the first two layers of subject analysis (description and identification). Identifying terms are in general more common than descriptive terms; it is very rare to find any terms at the third level of analysis. As with crowdsourcing, we do not see social networks involved in studying indexing level; technology, though, is involved in managing the experiments. As noticed in former studies the level of descriptors is concentrated on the generic level and the papers focus on improving this level. The connotative level seems very subjective and the users appreciate utilizing storytelling elements to improve this level.

Beaudoin (2016) communicated the findings of a case study that examined the methods used to develop visual literacy skills among 31 graduate students enrolled in a library and information science course. She employed the Detroit News Collection at Wayne State University where the Virtual Motor City is openly available. The overall pattern she observed in the development of richer image descriptions was that students struggled to perform the work well although they faced several obstacles. Some of their entries are incomplete or incorrect. Their ability to identify and assess the content of the images is limited. Developing visual literacy skills will help to provide students with a framework for analyzing picture content.

Table 2.8: Category Indexing with sub-category Metadata and Level of Description		
		Publication Per Year
Indexing—Metadata—Level of Description	2014: Klenczon and Rygiel;	1
	Rafferty and Albinfalah;	1
	Zeng, Graces, Žumer	1
	2016: Beaudoin	1

Motivation for the non-professional description of photos on social media shows that organizing for oneself is more common than organization for the public (social media). The motivation is personal communication with friends and family for two-third of the users, while one-third of the users' tags are for the public. Obar and Wildman (2015) wrote that "User-generated content is the lifeblood of social media" and it clearly demonstrates the advantage of supporting the users' benefit with added contacts via the social media. Research into users' tagging confirms that generic terms are more common in image descriptions than specific terms, and that abstract terms are rarely used. The benefits of indexing and retrieval can be difficult to separate. When comparing image tags with query terms on social media, the results show that there are clear similarities in the facets that are present in tags and in query terms, with terms relating to people and objects, or locations, being the most commonly used in both cases. This suggests that the aspects of images that users include in their image tags are the same as those that are of interest to users in their searches. Tags on images on social media that relate to generic objects and events show a high metadata usage ratio, while those related to specific locations and objects show a low ratio. Popular tags reflect the culture of the tagging population and serve as evidence of the social impact of collaborative social-tagging activities. Indexing research focuses on a blended indexing approach, which seems promising when deciding on image management and is in line with what was experienced in the LCs Flickr project (Springer et al., 2008). There is no doubt about the positive effect of user involvement in professional indexing.

2.5.3 SUB-CATEGORY GUIDELINES

The third sub-category under Indexing describes various means, which are useful for developing *Guidelines*. One issue is to look into the necessity for fostering simple rules for the users of various domains. Although major optimistic approaches have foreseen the development of additional algorithms for describing photos with an extension of CBIR, it seems that it is still a little premature.

Conduit and Rafferty (2007) produced an image-indexing template relevant for indexing by the Children's Society. The article describes a project that explores users' approaches to image retrieval, in the form of user queries recorded in published studies, in relation to the indexing practice and indexing wish lists of image archivists. Thirty-three archivists participated in the test where the Panofsky/Shatford (Armitage and Enser, 1997) matrix was used. The conclusion is that a matrix is an extremely useful framework through which to analyze and interpret specific features of images and provide a useful guideline in creating disciplined indexing. A ranked list of facets, which grew out of the research, proposes a practical tool for organizations wishing to construct their own indexing templates. However, during the course of the project it became clear that sometimes users' queries and archivists' wish lists do not match with the actual indexing practice undertaken. The reason for the gap between wish lists and practice relates speculatively to indexing tradition. Rorissa (2010) studied the question about similarities and differences between Flickr tags and controlled index terms used in general image collections. To test the query she used the content of 975 photos from Flickr and the University of St. Andrews Library Photographic Archive; the total of assigned tags was 4,159. The findings suggested that user tags and professionally assigned index terms have different underlying structures. Tags are given freely without any restrictions as to type and number, whereas professional indexers adhere to guidelines that define types and minimize the number of terms assigned. However, professionals may evaluate the contents of the information source more thoroughly than a Flickr tagger. The significance of research on the nature of social tagging and tags lies in the assumption that users will be likely to use similar, if not the same, terms during searching. Guidelines are not mentioned explicitly, and as the study has not continued, it is hard to draw any definite conclusion from the research.

A year later, Tang and Carter (2011) proposed a procedure for guiding people to create informative and descriptive alternative text for images and other graphical content. They developed a prototype tool based on the Panofsky/Shatford model and worked with four user groups, i.e., developers, accessibility specialists, content specialists, and Internet users. Two research studies evaluated the procedure in a document format and the prototype tool. Both evaluations confirmed the promise of this approach, and they identified several improvements to increase usability for guiding users. The same year Yoon and Chung (2011) used 474 questions obtained from a social question and answer (social Q&A) site. Their research was focused on attributes that expressed the daily image needs of ordinary users. They employed Wilson's (2006) model (which focuses on human use of information, rather than the use of information systems and sources), and the outcome showed that characteristics of each attribute and different types of image searches suggest that an image retrieval/indexing mechanism should not rely on a single approach. Different approaches (metadata, automatic indexing, professional indexing and user tags, and CBIR) are employed for enhanced keyword searching and browsing performance. The recommendation is for a kind of blended guidelines.

Matusiak (2013) studied the use of visual and multimedia resources in specific classroom contexts, such as lectures, discussion sections, and students' projects and assignments. She investigated 65 undergraduate students from a geography class at a large, public university in the U.S. The project, a case study, provides an in-depth description of the use of digital resources in a college classroom. The abundance of images and multimedia was evident in the class and met students' expectations. The subject matter offers itself to the use of visual materials, but the sheer amount of images in the observed class demonstrates that digital technology not only enables wider access to information resources, but also increases the possibilities for knowledge representation while providing a greater variety of educational resources.

Konkova et al. (2014) suggested that an alternative to professional image indexing can be social tagging. They examined whether social tagging can efficiently provide images with semantic descriptions, and how the social tagging behavior takes place in photo-sharing networks and image-labeling games. The first experiment operated on 130 top tags (collected from a tag cloud) and 500 tags (selected randomly) from the Flickr-based Content-based Photo Image Retrieval

(CoPhIR) test collection. Most of the user-assigned tags are by nature interpretive. The second experiment about a gaming application has shown to be slightly more perceptually oriented, as visual features (colors, shapes, and distinct objects) are easier to spot and match. However, specific guidelines can influence the game's outcome in order to obtain a given result. This shows that social tagging is a manageable process, but it depends on the taggers' understanding of the image use and on the nature of the tagging environment. The study shows that games are more oriented toward describing *what* in an image, while photo-sharing social networks present a more balanced picture of semantic facets, i.e., *what/where/when/who*. Guidelines are mentioned explicitly in this paper both for professional management and as a spillover for social networks.

Piras and Giacinto (2017) provide a somewhat futuristic and technical paper. They look at the techniques used to estimate the parameters of the query system to the interests of the users involved. The utilization of the Deep Learning Paradigm (DLP) is unfamiliar to the LIS field as it is rooted in computer science. It represents a different way of thinking and has recently attracted researchers in the computer vision community that dramatically advanced the state of image classification tasks by Neural Networks. The availability of more computing power, the strong popularity of deep learning approaches, as well as interest from a variety of actors will allow us to address issues like labeled data, feedback, interfaces, design fusion approaches, and guidelines with novel approaches that will leverage cooperation and knowledge sharing. Although the paper is quite technical, it provides some interesting insights about different descriptors.

Table 2.9: Category Indexing with sub-category Guidelines		
		Publication Per Year
Indexing—Metadata—Guidelines	2007: Conduit and Rafferty	1
	2010: Rorissa	1
	2011: Tang and Carter;	1
	Yoon and Chung	1
	2013: Matusiak	1
	2014: Konkova et al.	1
	2017: Piras and Giacinto	1

Summarizing the sub-category *Guidelines,* it is observed that user tags and professionally assigned index terms have different underlying structures. Tags are given freely without any restrictions as to type and number, whereas professional indexers adhere to guidelines that define types and minimize the number of terms assigned. However, professionals may evaluate the contents of the information source more thoroughly than a Flickr tagger. The significance of research on the nature of social tagging and tags lies in the assumption that users will be likely to use similar, if not identical, terms during searching. An alternative to professional image indexing can be social tagging. Most of the user-assigned tags are by nature interpretive, showing that social tagging is a manageable process, but it depends on the taggers' understanding of the image use and on the nature of the tagging environment.

2.5.4   SUB-CATEGORY EMOTIONS

The fourth sub-category *Emotions* concerns a specific aspect of image description, probably the most difficult one, as, according to Barthes (1964; 1969; 1980), it deals with subjective narratives. It is problematic to claim any objectivity dealing with individual interpretations of reality. In order to avoid the "un-professional" positivistic approach (Stewart, 2015), experiments geared toward finding a small number of emotional terms can be used by the indexer and have taggers provide emotive terms. Professional indexing deals with keywords and tags or un-controlled keywords. Tags given by users appear on LC's test collection of historical pictures on Flickr (Springer et al., 2008). The latter is doable because the work is done with a specific group of images, i.e., historic photos; however, not many experiments are done within such restricted areas. One methodology is to use quantitative tools for describing emotions, but even with CBIR low-level factual data is used. When it comes to contents, apart from such factual data as color, the results are unsuccessful.

Whether it is possible to index emotions consistently and use this information in retrieval systems are issues studied by Schmidt and Stock (2009). Their test collection consisted of 30 emotional photos from Flickr, and the participants in the test were 763 students from the Heinrich-Heine-University in Düsseldorf. The researchers followed an approach outlined by Lee and Neal (2007) in which they sought to determine whether the use of emotion-based, user-assigned descriptors, elicited from a Music Information Retrieval (MIR) system, can be employed. Schmidt and Stock found that for 17 out of the 30 photos, the test persons have clear emotional "favorites" when indexing. The question is, however, do users really need search systems that can perform searches for emotion? The study was limited in number of images and was very descriptive. Schmidt and Stock presented a popular idea: testing MIR from the field of music, where similar content description problems are involved. There is no follow-up to this study and researchers continue to focus on studying the content description for implying emotions. Neal (2010) presented her research that sought to improve emotion-based access to digital photographs. She examined tags for textual and visual elements communicating emotions. She used 300 photographs from Flickr from five categories: angry, sad, happy, afraid, and disgusting. Each category offered an alternative, i.e., being most or least relevant. The study presented some suggestions for discussion. Neal's conclusion was that, although we have learned nothing conclusive from the study, the concept and content of images are relevant for further study. Regretfully, no initiative followed the call for further research.

The same year, Yoon (2010) tested a new approach designed to enhance the accessibility of connotative messages, especially emotional meanings, during the image search process. This test involved two quantitative tools: (1) the Semantic Differential (SD)—a scale used for measuring the meaning of things and concepts and where the SD measures connotative meaning; and (2) the Self-Assessment Manikin (SAM)—an emotion-assessment tool that uses graphic scales, depicting cartoon characters expressing three emotion elements: pleasure, arousal, and dominance (Lund, 2016). She studied how the affective meanings of an image are represented by involving 58 students at the University of South Florida and utilizing 30 Creative Commons licensed images via Flickr. The photos are tagged with one of six basic emotions: love, joy, surprise, anger, sadness, or fear. The study's results demonstrated the potential of utilizing a quantitative measurement as an image-indexing mechanism that can enhance accessibility to emotional meanings of images. Through comparisons of quantitative measurements (SD and SAM) and three image-related tasks (searching, describing, and sorting), SAM is a potential means of representing emotional meanings of an image. Yoon (2011a) did not continue using quantitative tools to look for contents in images. Instead, she aimed to examine how to improve professional tools by exploring emotional perception of an image (again) through sorting, describing, and searching. This time 59 students were involved in the survey and Yoon's finding shows that there is only a relatively small number of emotional terms frequently chosen as descriptors or labels. When comparing image perceptions of an individual image across three tasks, overall similar perceptions are visible across the sorting, describing, and searching tasks. She therefore suggested assigning a small number of popular emotional terms to improve image retrieval effectiveness with minimum indexing efforts. Regretfully, there is no mention of how and by whom these emotional terms are to be developed. Yoon showed a different research strategy in handling professional photos; however, the suggestion has not been followed.

Table 2.10: Indexing Emotions		
		Publication Per Year
Indexing—Emotions	2009: Schmidt and Stock	1
	2010: Neal;	1
	Yoon	1
	2011a: Yoon	1

Summarizing the category *Emotions*, we note that social media are utilized in all the papers testing emotional categories. From 2009–2011, several excellent propositions for developing indexing (and retrieval) tools were published. Regrettably, none of the proposals have survived; they remain indexing and research "torsos". Table 2.11 illustrates all four sub-categories under Indexing.

Table 2.11: Category Indexing with four sub-categories: Collection Description, Metadata, Guidelines, and Emotions

		Publication Per Year
Indexing—Collection Description	2015: Harkema and Avery	1
Indexing—Metadada	2005: Enser, Sandom, and Lewis	1
	2007: Ames and Naaman;	1
	Jörgensen;	1
	Rafferty and Hidderley	1
	2009: Stvilia and Jörgensen;	1
	Yoon	1
	2010: Angus, Stuart, and Thelwall;	1
	Oden Nov and Chen Ye;	1
	Stvillia and Jörgensen	1
	2011: Ransom and Raferty;	1
	Terras	1
	2012: Beaudoin;	1
	Estellés-Arolas and González-Ladrón-de-Guevara;	1
	Petek;	1
	Stvillia, Jörgensen, and Wu	1
	2013: Fauzi and Belkhatir;	1
	Huang and Jörgensen;	1
	Jörgensen, Stvilia, and Wu	1
	2014: Drew and Guillemin;	1
	Fauzi and Belkhatir;	1
	Klenczon and Rygiel;	1
	Kovács and Takács;	1
	Nakatsu, Grossman, and Iacovou;	1
	Rafferty and Albinfalah;	1
	Zeng, Graces, and Žumer	1
	2015: Benson;	1
	Lin et al.	1
	2016: Beaudoin	1

Indexing—Guidelines	2007: Conduit and Rafferty	1
	2010: Rorissa	1
	2011: Tang and Carter;	1
	Yoon and Chung	1
	2013: Matusiak	1
	2014: Konkova et al.	1
	2017: Piras and Giacinto	1
Indexing—Emotions	2009: Schmidt and Stock	1
	2010: Neal;	1
	Yoon	1
	2011: Yoon(a)	1

2.6   CATEGORY RETRIEVAL

The category *Retrieval* contains five sub-categories (see Figure 2.7) representing different facets. The first two sub-categories *Framework* and *CBIR* are about accessing image information, and the final three, *Queries*, *Taxonomy*, and *User Needs*, deal with how users request information, models for retrieval categories, and functions that influence the search. The researchers predominantly use qualitative approaches. There are, however, differences in the various qualitative procedures. Qualitative methods described everything from assessing models to questionnaires and interviews to named devices (Brinkman and Kvale, 2015).

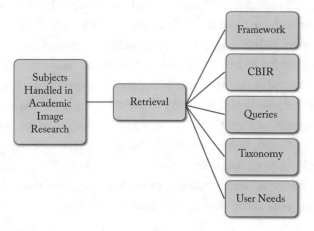

Figure 2.7: Code, category, and sub-categories for Retrieval.

What is the motivation for retrieving images?

Mette Sandbye

Looking into what I call everyday images on social media is either about connecting and communicating with friends and family, or in the case where you look at private images on blogs, Facebook, or Instagram, you can be motivated by a need for aesthetics or a more psychological need, as already mentioned, to mirror yourself through other people's images. If we turn to the media, for instance, the speed of modern media production, including constantly feeding into web versions, makes it tempting to retrieve photos from photo agencies, stock companies, or even private sources on the Internet. Source criticism comes under pressure and is sometimes sacrificed in this high-speed, click-hunting approach. Likewise, often the same kinds of images, even the very same image, are being distributed. Thus, paradoxically, we lose nuances in our visual narration of history and society.

2.6.1   SUB-CATEGORY FRAMEWORK

Rafferty and Hidderley (2007) presented three models in a reflective, though experimental paper about expert-led, author-generated, and user-orientated information retrieval (IR). The testbed was Flickr and indexing and retrieval were done by the Democratic Indexing Project (Hidderley and Rafferty, 1997). The intention for use in a dynamic retrieval system is to allow users to contribute to the indexing and retrieval process. By focusing on user interpretation, Democratic Indexing differs from traditional IR models, which assume that retrieval mechanisms are constructed by the librarian/indexer. Flickr and the Democratic Indexing Project from 2007 are examples of systems offering alternatives (as we write) to traditional semantic structures. Choices regarding *Knowledge Organization* tools and methods are dependent on the format and content of the signs, and the function of the retrieval activity. Another reflective paper is presented by Enser et al. (2007) where they investigated whether low-level, syntactic properties of an image have a practical value or if it is limited to a few specialized applications. They argued that users' interest in images lies with their inferred semantic content; and a retrieval facility, which returns candidate images lacking in semantic integrity, has little or no operational value. The recommendation for the next generation of truly capable semantic image retrieval systems is to further integrate automatic indexing techniques and intellectual indexing harnessing domain and tacit knowledge.

Rosch et al. (1976) were the first to compile and articulate basic-level categories. According to them, human perceptions have three levels of categorization. The basic level is the level where most people tend naturally to categorize an issue/item. Categories exist at various levels, described as *basic*, *subordinate*, and *superordinate*. Subordinate categories are more specific than their basic category, and superordinate categories more general. A commonly utilized example is Chair—Basic level, Rocking chair—Subordinate level, and Furniture—Superordinate level. Rorissa (2008) utilized the basic-level categories in his research where he focused on a hierarchical and widely used framework (Figure 2.8). The Basic-level theory and its three levels of abstraction (subordinate, basic, and superordinate) are employed to compare descriptions of individual images and labels of groups of images.

Superordinate-level terms are more generic than a given basic-level term.	Basic-level terms are more specific than a given superordinate-level term.	Subordinate-level terms are more specific than a given basic-level term.
• Are more generic and plural than specific and singular • Are terms for which one can think of several manifestations (examples) • Describe objects that share few common features and have more distinctive features • Describe more abstract or functional features • Describe groups, collections, or classes of objects • Are terms with at least four levels beneath them (in WordNet) • Convey more relational information (e.g., relative location) • Convey both functional information and general knowledge about the objects they refer to, e.g., vehicle, furniture, food, work, style, personality, crime, transportation, housework	• Are singular rather than plural • Are shorter (15 or fewer characters long) and usually consist of one or two words • Are not phrases • Are included within the names of more specific terms (e.g., car in "sports car", shirt in "dress shirt") • Are more informative and they identify/reference single objects/features • Describe objects that share relatively more common features and are relatively similar • Describe concrete and perceptual entities (entities that can be perceived through the senses and mentally represented in a single image) • Describe salient features • Make distinctions or distinguish one object from another • Convey information on the parts and components of objects, e.g., car, chair	• Are formed from a basic-level term and a modifier • Are compound and/or phrases (e.g., department store, dress shirt, sports car) • Have no children (in WordNet) • Refer to specific examples and/or single objects • Describe a particular kind of basic-level object • Convey information concerning the superficial properties of the objects they refer to, such as texture and color, e.g., sedan

Figure 2.8: Coding scheme, level Definition (Rorissa, 2008).

Rorissa (2008) concentrated on two studies on 50 digital images from the Hemera Photo Objects Volume I (stock photo collection of over 50,000 images). In a third study, he considered 30 photographs included in O'Connor and Wyatt's (2004) book. The number of participants was 30 in the first study, 75 in the second, and 75 again in the third study. His aim was to discover whether the Basic-level theory provides possible solutions to a number of problems ranging from browsing interfaces to standardization of taxonomies and labeling of categories. While a taxonomy based on the three levels would fit most current taxonomies in terms of the number of levels of depth, the results of the three reported studies show something different. For browsing purposes labels for individual images and their objects can be at the basic level while labels for groups of images can be at the superordinate level. Rorissa's choice of the Basic-level theory is justified by previous similar studies by LIS researchers. Rorissa and Iyer (2008) again employed the Basic-level theory to understand human categorization as it is essential to user-centered design of taxonomies, ontologies, browsing interfaces, and other indexing tools and systems. They included the data from the three studies mentioned above. Results of the first two studies revealed that user-supplied image category labels are predominantly at the superordinate level. Subordinate-level category labels were hardly used by participants. Similar previous studies on the nature of categorization of images strongly support these results. Social tagging may prove to be an alternative to professional indexing and/or may serve as a complement to professional indexing. The basic-level categories applied and used across different domains have been identified in image indexing and retrieval.

Hajibayova's (2013) paper discusses an application of Heidegger's notion of handiness as a framework for understanding the relational nature of the basic-level categories. The theory is employed in LIS where research has been confined to two questions about how the basic level of categories is represented in *Knowledge Organization* systems, and how basic-level terms are used to represent the conceptual content of resources, i.e., images (Rorissa and Iyer, 2008). Hajibayova suggests using the universality of the basic-level categories to build crosswalks between classificatory systems and user-centered indexing. The basic-level categories vary across individuals and cultures because of differences in the everyday experiences and activities of individuals.

Table 2.12: Category Retrieval with sub-category Framework		
		Publication Per Year
Retrieval—Framework	2008: Rorissa;	1
	Rorissa and Iyer	1
	2013: Hajibayova	1

Summarizing the sub-category *Framework*, the research strategies reflect solutions to retrieval by providing abstract representations, connected to the research project's goal, that direct the collection and analysis of data. Deliberations of the studies are open-ended and the articles work as contextual resources for more recent papers about image retrieval.

What is the motivation for retrieving images?

Mette Kia Krabbe Meyer

If we want to see how the National Socialists used images in their propaganda, study how Nazi Germany was depicted in the press in the 1930s. If we want to see how amateurs documented their lives, we look at newspapers, print material, photo albums, etc. If historians a hundred years from now want to look at the way our present is depicted, they will be searching digital material. It is not easy to foresee how this search is going to take place, but a condition for this retrieval is that the material has been saved. In Denmark, the Royal Danish Library has been collecting all printed material for centuries under the Legal Deposit Law. Since 2005, this has included the Danish part of the Internet, too. All .dk sites are harvested on a quarterly basis and the harvesting is regularly supplemented (see more at netarkivet.dk/in-english/). News sites consist of ever-changing input from a lot of sources and are a lot more complex than print newspapers. But digital media also holds a lot of information, which we did not have earlier on. We can easily trace images as they appear in different contexts and we can track comments on the images, too. This means that research into the social meaning of images can be done in new ways with new material and new tools. A hundred years ago the science of photo astronomy developed as a consequence of the fact that photography was included in the investigation of space. It meant that astronomers had to know a lot about photochemistry when they used photography as a tool. Likewise, the historian in the future will have to know a lot about the sharing, storing, and retrieval of images if they want to study the role of images in different historical contexts. In the library, specialists in digital preservation work to make sure that not only are images saved but that they can also be viewed decades from now when software and hardware have changed. I, too, take part in the efforts to improve principles of harvesting and I am engaged in the current exploration of image proliferation and interpretation in the digital era.

2.6.2   CBIR

Beaudoin (2015) studied the knowledge of and perceptions about content-based image retrieval among several professional user groups. Here the investigation is whether or not knowledge about CBIR technologies is reaching groups of users whose work tasks involve images. She included 20 professional participants representing archaeology, art history, architecture, and the artistic fields in the test. Given that CBIR technologies have occupied researchers over several decades, there is an obvious need to determine if users know about these methods, and if and how CBIR technologies may be applied by them in practice. The findings of this study suggest that CBIR retrieval methods are likely to be more readily adopted among individuals interested in finding images based on their formal characteristics. Interest in CBIR methods varied among the different professional user communities. Individuals who showed an interest in these systems were primarily those concerned with searching for the formal characteristics in images. Mounika et al. (2016) also studied the process of digitization and concluded that image collections are not, as such, easier to manage. Some form of cataloging and indexing is still necessary, the only difference being that much of the required information can now potentially be derived automatically from the images themselves. In contrast to the text-based approach of the systems described above, CBIR operates on a totally different principle, retrieving stored images from a collection by comparing features like color, texture, or shape automatically extracted from the images themselves. The main advantage of this paper is that the authors proved that they can retrieve images based on both the color features and the texture features at the same time.

Table 2.13: Category Retrieval with sub-category CBIR		
		Publication Per Year
Retrieval—CBIR	2015: Beaudoin	1
	2016: Mounika et al.	1

Summarizing the sub-category *CBIR,* one paper contemplates that CBIR functions in work areas where the search is for factual items in an image. The second paper does not report on any difficulty involved in CBIR searching. However, an interesting perspective is the comment about *digitalization not in itself making image collections easier to manage* (Mounika et al., 2016, p. 4331). It is important to realize that digitization solves no problem—the problem has to be solved before any digitization.

2.6.3   SUB-CATEGORY QUERIES

Jansen (2008) studied efficient mapping of web image queries, and investigated whether the mapping can use previously identified image classification schemes by Enser and McGregor (1992), Jörgensen (1998), and Chen (2001). His testing showed that none of the above classification schemes captured the richness of web image searching. From these results, he derived a scheme for classifying web image queries either manually or by automatic meta-tagging. One immediate implementation will be for the meta-tagging of queries to meet these new classifiers and to develop interfaces to support such searching in image collections. He recommended the design and development of effective image retrieval systems based on real users' search for digital images. A year later, Chung and Yoon (2009) analyzed the differences between user-supplied tags and search queries for images in terms of categories and levels of specificity. An overall distribution of categories and levels of specificity demonstrated to be similar among user-supplied tags and search query terms. The generic category is the most frequently used for both tags and search query terms. Following the generic category, the specific and abstract categories were next in frequency. This result is similar to Rorissa and Iyer's (2008) finding about the predominant use of the superordinate level. However, it is dissimilar to their discovery of the subordinate level hardly used by participants. The color category turned out as the least-used category.

Mounika et al. (2016) presented a different conclusion about the color category in image retrieval; however, Chung and Yoon (2009) focused on the textual description and not on data extracted by algorithms. Precision in image retrieval was studied by Peters and Stock (2010) by testing if precision could be enhanced by the use of power tags, which are document-specific terms shared by a broad spectrum of people (see Figure 2.9 and Vander Wal, 2005).

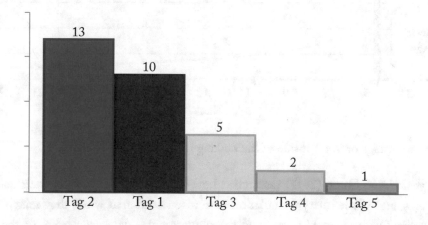

Figure 2.9: Tag distribution (www.vanderwal.net/random/entrysel.php?blog=1635).

The aim is to cut off all tags in the long tail of a document-specific tag distribution. The remaining tags (at the beginning of a tag distribution) are considered power tags and form a new, additional search option in information retrieval systems (see Figure 2.10). The basic idea of power tags is to "harvest" the tags on the left-hand side of the distribution as particularly important document tags. Based on the findings, the paper presents a sketch of an algorithm for mining and processing power tags in information search systems. Choi and Hsieh-Yee (2010) examined characteristics of user search queries for image retrieval and compared the retrieval effectiveness of subject headings and description notes in supporting user image queries in an OPAC system. Thirty-three students and recent graduates of a library and information science program were involved in the test, using one photo and one poster from the Library of Congress Prints and Photographs Online

Catalog. The subject domain and the format of images seem to influence query development. Additionally, the study found that neither subject headings nor description notes are very successful in supporting user queries for images.

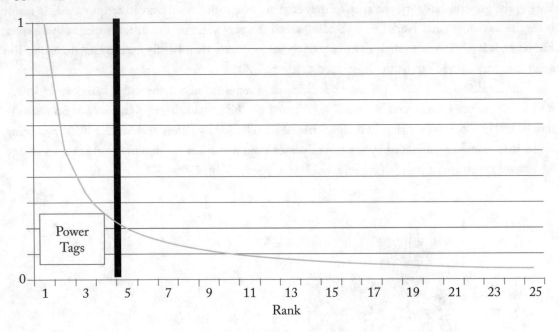

Figure 2.10: Power tags on the left side of the ranking (Peters and Stock, 2010).

Two years later, Hung (2012) researched how photo editors formulate their queries for retrieving images, and if the query formulation patterns are different when they search for specific, general, or subjective images. He examined the photo archive database system of the Associated Press (AP), and the participants were 30 photo editors. The study revealed that query formulation, and especially query reformulation, are the difficult tasks that the searchers face, especially for the subjective image search. The study suggests establishing a sensitive and responsive thesaurus system, whose display of synonymous and hierarchical terms may help searchers construct their queries more correctly and more efficiently. Choi (2013) surveyed the relationship between query-modification patterns and contextual factors to explore the semantic attributes of image searching incorporated by users when formulating a query during information retrieval. In her test, she employed 978 image search queries and 29 college students at the Department of Media Studies. She found that participants frequently incorporate format-related terms and contextual information related to the image. Moreover, she discovered that participants tend to compose an initial query with specific information and contextual information, such as bibliographic information or information related to production of the image.

Table 2.14: Category Retrieval with sub-category Queries		
		Publication Per Year
Retrieval—Queries	2008: Jansen	1
	2009: Chung and Yoon	1
	2010: Choi and Hsieh-Yee;	1
	Peters and Stock	1
	2012: Hung	1
	2013: Choi	1
	2015: Park et al.	1

Summarizing the sub-category *Queries,* the research concentrates on user query categorization and extension of image information. Retrieval and tagging are studied and a preliminary result is to employ user queries as improved tools for image retrieval. Images from social media are not involved in the experiments.

What is the motivation for retrieving images?

Louise Broch

There are more reasons for photo retrieval. The Danish Broadcasting Corporation (DR) utilizes photographs every day to supplement the articles on dr.dk. Still photographs are used to provide perspectives to the documentary programs. Still photographs and videos complement each other; however, still photographs function in some ways better than videos because they capture and sustain emotions. Every time you utilize an image the photograph must be cleared for copyright. This process can be rather lengthy and sometimes a bit tedious.

2.6.4   SUB-CATEGORY (QUERY) TAXONOMY

Basic levels of description for online photographs were investigated by Lee and Neal (2010), utilizing the Hierarchy for Online Photograph Representation (HOPR) model. The representation is based on a need for a model that addresses users' basic levels of photograph description and retrieval. The test implies 16 (private) photos and 138 library science graduate students. Some general observations are that objects and events taking place in the photograph are the most commonly used levels of description. UADs for image indexing and retrieval pinpoint the shortcomings of the HOPR model and suggestions are to test an edited version that has further refinement.

Many studies have indicated the difficulty of indexing image *Aboutness* (Lancaster, 2003) due to its subjective characteristics. The findings in this study emphasize the importance of a "down-top" approach instead of a "top-down" approach. Applying UADs for tagging photographs online is a "down-top" approach, allowing many users to contribute their knowledge. Tirilly et al. (2012) addressed defining image similarity and examined if humans assess image similarity in the same way. Thirty-five persons, recruited from the general population through flyers, emails, posters, and snowball sampling, examined 40 pairs of images from MIRFlickr. The results showed that the subjects do not have collective strategies of similarity assessment but that a satisfying consensus can be found individually on the data samples used in the experiments. The authors proposed methods to define reference similarity scores and rankings based on this. These methods can be used on a larger scale to produce realistic ground truths for the evaluation of image-retrieval systems.

Maniu et al. (2013) analyzed user actions during search sessions conducted on a large photo-sharing platform. Search accounts for a significant part of user interactions with such platforms, and the study showed differences between the queries issued on photo-sharing platforms and those on general image search. The study used Flickr web server logs of user behavior during the entire search sessions. A query taxonomy for image search, which makes distinctions between general and specific queries, pointed to general queries being the most frequent category. However, the percentage of general queries was less than reported by Jansen (2008) in the sub-category Queries. The authors show that the query type influences search behavior, and depends on the user, too.

Park et al. (2015) analyzed users' image search behavior on a large-scale query log from Yahoo Image Search, based on the conclusion of a study from 2013 about behavior being dependent on query type. For categorization of the queries the authors use two taxonomies, i.e., International Press Telecommunications Council (IPTC) subject code taxonomy (2017) and Panofsky/Shatford Categorization Rules. The conclusion indicates important behavioral differences across query types, in particular showing that some query types are more exploratory, while others correspond to focused search. They supplemented the study with a survey to link the behavioral differences to image search intent. The findings shed light on the importance of considering query categories to understand user behavior on image search platforms.

Göker et al. (2016) presented a study about development of an image- retrieval system that is not simply a derivative of a document-retrieval system. It emphasized the differences between images and documents. The aim of their paper was to characterize the image-seeking behavior of professional image searchers. Thirteen participants, of whom ten were image consumers, participated in the test. In most of the tasks the authors observed that the images sought were not an information end in themselves, and that they accompanied text and information in other media. The images were retrieved to fulfill one or more of the following three forms of image use: to give the overall document more impact (emotive/persuasive purposes); to illustrate information in the document (illustration); and to improve the aesthetics of the document (aesthetic value). The outcome of the study was a set of design recommendations that question whether the document-retrieval model that most search engines are based on, i.e., keywords go in, and a linear list of about

20 results is appropriate for image retrieval. Konkova, MacFarlane, and Göker (2016) investigated "briefs", which are a very detailed ways of describing an image need along with giving a well-specified context of use. Analysis of a brief can serve as a basis for development of a new image-search approach. The research is about developing search facet schemes for image search engines, and discovering whether they cater to user needs. The authors interviewed the same 13 participants (as described above) about the facets, and the outcome was a set of search facets for an image system for creative professionals. The facets do not act as a conventional search engine based on keyword queries but actually as part of a brief creation tool that will support the information needs of a user with a more detailed and contextually rich description of images.

Table 2.15: Category Retrieval with sub-category Taxonomy		
		Publication Per Year
Retrieval—Taxonomy	2007: Rafferty and Hidderly	1
	2010: Lee and Neal	1
	2012: Tirilly et al.	1
	2013: Maniu et al.	1
	2016: Göker et al.;	1
	Konkova, MacFarlane, and Göker	1

Summarizing the sub-category *Taxonomy*, suggestions for actual query categorizations are presented. The papers provide an evaluation tool for image similarities and a template of query categories grouping query types. The results are relevant for further development of automatic retrieval. Another approach is the development of a set of search facets for an image search system for creative professionals, and design recommendations that question the document-retrieval model that most search engines are based on.

How do you predict the image to be retrieved in the (near) future?

Mette Kia Krabbe Meyer

At present, only researchers have access to the net archive. Images are retrieved by free text searching, and this applies as well to our digital collections in which singular images are stored with metadata. In this respect, the library works in collaboration with other archives and with users providing metadata that enriches the collections. Different solutions are explored for automatically generated metadata, etc. In the near future, I expect retrievals to be text based, but of course the library takes interest in employing different kinds of image recognition tools as well. If possible, they will be applied to the retrieval of images in our digital collections and in the net archive.

2.6.5   USER NEEDS

Andre et al. (2009) explored the differences between image and general web search to better support users' needs. As seen above, the majority of search engines have a keyword query followed by a paginated, ranked list of results. The authors interviewed eight researchers, designers, and managers about their understanding of the unique characteristics and usage of image search, which can contribute to the design of a focused and compelling image search experience. First, they offered a qualitative and quantitative analysis of differences in behavior between image and web search; second, they used those insights to ground recommendations for the design of image search; and then they iterated on a number of designs and built a functional prototype. These concepts are only a few examples in a world of potential new designs in image search done within computer science.

Yoon (2011b) investigated image users' needs and search queries in their daily lives, including both personal and school- and work-related environments. Fifty-eight undergraduate and graduate students answered a web survey questionnaire investigating what, where, why, and how college students search images. Students preferred their familiar web search engines to specialized image archives and databases. The searchers' preference for web search engines corresponded to image needs that included associated information along with the image itself.

Chung and Yoon (2011) examined how Image needs are interwoven with intended uses. Their survey examined users' 192 image-seeking questions from a web-based Yahoo social Q&A service. The findings of this study provide an understanding of users' needs in relation to image use, which is one of the significant contextual factors affecting users' image needs and search behaviors. Users are likely to seek images using abstract attributes when they intend to use images as sources of objects, and specific attributes when using the images as sources of data. The University of Houston Digital Library (UHDL) provided the high-resolution images from 2014. Image delivery is an automated system called the Digital Cart Service. An unexpected benefit of the system is the reporting mechanism that produces data that includes intended use information.

Reilly and Thompson (2014) discussed the analysis of this data to determine why images are used, what products the images can create, and what implications this has on digital library management. The researchers found that specific user groups used images for different purposes depending on their work, needs, and research areas. Visitors, the largest user group, were downloading images (particularly maps and photographs) for their own personal collections. Images were downloaded to decorate home and office spaces, to enrich genealogical research and family history, and to celebrate important life moments. A study by Albertson (2015) synthesized research throughout different, yet complementary, areas, each capable of contributing findings and understanding to visual information seeking. Reviews of visual information need focus on query formulations. The paper reported on the findings and understanding about the visual information-seeking process stemming from a range of studies that employs a diverse set of methods. Similar to prior research in other information-seeking areas, the visual process has been investigated as task specific, starting with a need (many times made up by researchers), retrieval of items or information that may or may not satisfy a search topic, and concluding the session, such as by selecting information or not (Ingwersen, 1992; Ingwersen and Järvelin, 2005). Visual information, because of its multidimensional makeup, is relevant to examine specifically for its potential to advance other information and collaborative processes and outcomes.

Table 2.16: Category Retrieval with sub-category User Needs		
		Publication Per Year
Retrieval—User Needs	2007: Enser et al.	1
	2009: Andre et al.	1
	2011: Chung and Yoon;	1
	Yoon (2011b)	1
	2014: Reilly and Thompson	1
	2015: Albertson	1

Summarizing the sub-category *User Needs*, the research is a bit similar to the report for the sub-category *Taxonomy*. However, the observation addresses the users and not so much an improvement of a system. Users stick to what they appreciate, and the results show that their appreciation sub-divides according to intended utilization, be it work, requirement, or research fields.

How do you predict the image to be retrieved in the (near) future?

Mette Sandbye

The more images we produce, the more we need platforms and programs that cannot only archive them but can also make us search for and find them. When I "image-google" a phenomenon I have a certain amount of images of it in a second. Technology has provided possibilities of image retrieval we could never have dreamt of 20 years ago. But Facebook and Google administer by algorithms as well, which are difficult to understand for ordinary people and control what kind of images we are presented with. We should therefore be aware of what we do not find, when we google, or which political or social situations or conflicts we do not meet in the visual representation in the media.

It is interesting how a traditional press photograph can be disseminated/spread within a few hours on a global scale—via social media. An example could be the photograph of the drowned Syrian boy Aylan Kurdi on a beach in Turkey in September 2015. Several academic studies have shown the enormous high-speed spread of this one particular photograph taken by photographer Nilufer Demir. A specific study looked into the newspaper coverage of the Syrian refugee crisis before, immediately after, and a week after this specific image. It showed that the media coverage accelerated immensely due to this photograph. However, a week later the media attention was below the level it had been before the incident.

So images, easily retrieved on the Internet, connect people. They can make us see and understand conflicts and incidents on a global scale, but at the same time we must be aware of who controls this image flood. This is also a task for academic researchers today.

We are confronted with the differences between user-supplied tags and search queries for images on social media in terms of categories and levels of specificity. An overall distribution demonstrates similarity among user-supplied tags and search query terms. We see that the generic category is the most frequently used for both tags and search query terms, followed by the specific and abstract categories. This result is similar to Rorissa and Iyer's (2008) finding about the predominant use of the superordinate level. Van der Wal (2005) introduces power tags and reiterates the basic idea of power tags, that is to "harvest" the tags on the left-hand side of the distribution (see Figure 2.10) as particularly important document tags. Based on the findings, an algorithm for mining and processing power tags in information search systems can be presented. Another idea is to apply UADs for tagging photographs online as a "down-top" approach, allowing many users to contribute their knowledge.

2.7   SUMMARY

In the literature study the references from 2005–2017 is accessed to understand which "… academic image research areas [were] undertaken since the emergence of social media." Only one social medium, Flickr, is utilized in many studies and presumably the reason is the fewer copyright restrictions on Flickr photos. Another observation is that many of the test persons are students, and of them, several take library and information science courses. Looking at the research areas we notice that papers selected by using PRISMA leave out predominantly technical articles and documents primarily concentrating on art paintings. Grounded Theory is used for analyzing and the main category/code outlines a kind of empirical road map and suggests sub-categories. The 71 peer-reviewed conference and journal articles in English are arranged in three categories, i.e., *Domains*, *Indexing*, and *Retrieval*.

The research papers in the first category, *Domains*, denote that there is no major change in the endorsed study after the introduction of social media. The research shows that students in the tests prefer generic tags in the domains, and that metadata only slightly influences the results. Many traditional methodologies were used after the advent of social media. However, new research areas suggest analyzing the visual content in images and considering different professionals' requirements.

The results of the literature review indicate that taggers, utilizing the Panofsky/Shatford model, are interested in more than the pre-iconographic subject matter that professional indexers focus on. There is a general trend suggesting to categorize images, to work with guidelines and tag clouds, and to encourage UADs. Taggers can enhance the subject indexing provided by professionals, and training interventions significantly affect how taggers tag the content found in, e.g., historical photographs. The various journalistic media have individual classifications based on attributes in the photo, and when it comes to retrieval there is a suggestion to browse by separate attributes. Guidelines are presented as positive and essential especially for new employees. Professionals from different fields have different ways of employing images. Within domains the management of visual content is not equally important for all areas.

Indexing is the dominant class when it comes to the number of chosen research papers. Indexing and retrieval complement each other, and their separation in this lecture is solely based on our discretion. In the category *Indexing* there are four sub-categories where the scope of the first three sub-categories is generic while the fourth is specific.

Collection Description is the first of the sub-categories and it contains only one paper about practical collection management; however, no special research strategy is presented about how to deal with professional photos. Commercial interests, however, are mentioned, and it may be of interest to, e.g., private stock photo archives.

Metadata is the second sub-category and includes papers divided into five parameters. The *Semantic Gap* involves the difference between a human description of visual media and a machine description of the same. At the beginning of the study period in 2005, much writing was about manual annotations and the necessity of enhancing the functionality of current automatic annotation techniques. There was a call for new paradigms to take shape; however, there is no major change in the research after the introduction of the social media. Different surveys about *models* focus on a blended indexing approach and the findings concentrate on what to accomplish with photos, particularly on Flickr. Researchers consider new categories that Flickr users can employ for development of digital photo collections, and study Flickr photos as academic image resources in different subjects. Social networks are the focus of research, and academics concentrate solely on social media. *Motivation for Tagging* is touched upon in many research papers and the topic is divided into private and professional areas. Starting with the private fields there is the question about "laziness", i.e., point-of-capture for example on the mobile device, which is a new subject to be considered. Personal motivation is communication with friends and family while tagging is seen as more of an organizational issue for the public. A special case is to use photographs to show what it is like to live with an ongoing health condition, and actions taken to care about your health. In general, both social presence and individual level motivations affect users' tagging level. Professional topics touch upon editing classification schemes and thesauri, and tests about user-supplied tags and those applied to thesaurus design. Research articles also focus on basic-level theory where descriptors indicate basic-level terms, and the question about how to include frequently used superordinate- and subordinate-level terms. One paper indicates a need for greater inclusion of specific category terms, which are important in thesaurus revision especially when establishing related tags. In contrast, other professional initiatives are devoted to limitations on numbers and types of relationships allowed in controlled vocabularies. The *Motivation for Tagging* papers do not question previous assumptions but consider new research questions, and social networks are the nucleus of study. The *Value of Tags* demonstrates that generic terms are more commonly used in image descriptions than specific terms, and that abstract terms are rarely used. The most popular tags relate to generic objects and events and they show a high metadata usage ratio, while a low ratio appears when the tags relate to specific locations and objects. Popular tags on Flickr appear less frequently as image metadata when describing specific objects. Results show that a mix of tags can be more helpful for image search than one of these conditions alone. It also appears that image tags describe the same properties and facets of an image as those utilized in image queries. This may suggest that the aspects of images that users include in their image tags are the same as those that are of interest to users in their search queries. The findings of this study indicate that several quality criteria of image indexing are different from those of textual document indexing, such as context, moods, importance, and level of detail. It shall be added that there is a growing attention to reviewing digital images in cultural and heritage materials. *Editing Classification Schemes and Thesauri* study user-supplied tags and how they can be applied to designing a thesaurus that reflects the unique features of image documents. Shatford's facet category (1986; Layne, 1994) and Rosch et al.'s (1976) basic-level theory are evaluated to suggest concepts to be included in a thesaurus. The results show that the best approach, especially for "color" and "generic" category descriptors, is to focus on basic-level terms and only occasionally to include superordinate- and subordinate-level terms (see Figure 2.8). Complementing the controlled vocabulary terms with social terms more than doubled the average coverage of participants' terms for a photograph. There is no doubt about the positive effect by user involvement in indexing. "Taking the pictures to the people" has resulted in reaching large new audiences (Springer et al., 2008). A significant amount of time and labor has already gone into building image-indexing systems used in large-scale enterprises. Two of the better-known controlled vocabularies are the TGM and the Art and Architecture Thesaurus (AAT).

Crowdsourcing, the wisdom of the crowd, is a recent method of of indexing. There are research papers on definitions of crowdsourcing and frameworks for development of a taxonomy on crowdsourcing based on the literature on task complexity and the study of virtual teams. An automatic semantic analysis tool is developed utilizing Panofsky's three-layer theory, and the conclusion is that entities and tags correspond almost exclusively to the first two layers of subject analysis (pre-iconography and iconography). It is very rare to find any terms at his iconology level of analysis. Other studies claim that text-based search techniques (and thereby indexing) remain the most efficient and accurate methods for image retrieval. However, there is a need for developing visual literacy skills. Even within crowdsourcing, narratives are tested to design a story-based image-indexing system. Differences in interpretation are likely to come at the connotative level (see Figure 1.1) and, at this level, storytelling might offer a particularly rich input method. *Level of Description* is the study of which level should be adapted for images, and the indexing tool(s) for successful use. Low-level properties of an image, such as shape, texture, and color, contribute to the understanding of an image, but do not define it, and, according to research results, text-based search techniques remain the most efficient and accurate methods for image retrieval. As noticed in former studies, the level of descriptors is concentrated at the generic level and the focus is on improving this level. The connotative level seems very subjective and users appreciate utilizing storytelling elements to improve this level.

The articles in the third sub-category, *Guidelines,* describe ideas for the development of guiding principles, although rules for image-indexing templates are also proposed. There is a special focus on practical tools for organizations wishing to construct their own indexing templates. However, guidelines seem to have different underlying structures. Tests demonstrate that user tags are assigned freely without any restrictions as to types and numbers, whereas professional indexers adhere to guidelines that define types and minimize the number of terms assigned. The test results concern similarities and differences between Flickr taggers' tags and controlled index terms used in general image collections. A process is presented for guiding people to create informative and descriptive alternative text for images. These principles clarify which attributes of image context and content are expressed in ordinary users' daily image needs. Blended guidelines presented in 2011 are used as the basis for development of novel approaches in the computer science field in 2017. However, the Panofsky/Shatford model is still used when testing various proposals for new guidelines.

Academic papers from the fourth and last sub-category, *Emotions,* are on a specific level. Although one researcher asks if users really need search systems that can perform searches for emotion, all other papers take it for granted that there is this need, and concentrate on indexing emotions consistently. There is a strong belief that emotion-based access to digital photographs can be improved by connotative messages, especially emotional meanings and perceptions through sorting, describing, and searching an image. One test indicates that only a small number of emotional terms appear as descriptors, and it is suggested to assign a small number of popular emotional terms to improve indexing. The connotative message or level is rather difficult, and one study tested the system MIR—from the music area—where similar content description problems are involved. An automatic approach tested the software Self-Assessment Manikin (SAM) which demonstrates possibilities for representing emotional meanings of an image. Regretfully, there is no follow-up to this study.

How do you predict the image to be retrieved in the (near) future?

Louise Broch

Although the users utilize each other's knowledge and correct each other in a positive way when they tag, the librarian's expertise is essential even though the performance of the fast search engines can assist you. I perceive the librarian's role today more as that of a curator than an information specialist. In DR we still have problems with emotional terms since they are not a part of metadata. It is tedious to look for a broadcast with laughing people when emotional terms are not used for tagging. The cultural heritage database users, though, employ emotional tags. Crowdsourcing people (mostly retirees) have more time than employees do, and they take pleasure in their vocation. Some of the cultural heritage tags are given by former broadcasting staff. They know about photos, are still interested in the subjects, and as the organization is short staffed they are a great help. I have certainly had positive experiences with the crowdsourcing group.

The third category, *Retrieval,* has the largest number of sub-categories but not the largest number of academic papers. Contrary to what is seen in the category *Indexing,* these sub-categories are at the same level. Papers from the first sub-category, *Framework,* concern basic-level categories. The universality of these categories is used to build connections between classificatory systems and user-centered indexing, and it provides an understanding of human categorization. Tests recommend that labels for individual images and their objects can be at the basic level, while labels for groups of images can be at the superordinate level. The subordinate level, however, is hardly used by participants. Deliberations of the studies are open-ended and the articles are used as contextual resources for more recent papers about image retrieval. Studies about *CBIR,* the second sub-category, are about work in areas where the search is mostly for factual items in an image. It operates on different principles retrieving stored images from a collection by comparing features like color, texture, or shape automatically extracted from the images themselves. Knowledge about CBIR technologies is reaching groups of users whose work tasks involve images. However, the tests indicate that individuals who demonstrate an interest in these systems are primarily concerned with searching for the formal characteristics in images. The papers in the third sub-category, *Queries,* focus on design and development of effective image retrieval systems based on actual users' searches for digital images. Query formulation and especially query reformulation are the difficult tasks, and a thesaurus system is proposed to be established for a display of synonymous and hierarchical terms, which may help searchers construct their queries more correctly and efficiently. Test results show that format-related terms and contextual information related to the image are important, though subject domains and format of images also seem to influence query development. Power tags form a new, additional search option in information retrieval systems, and one paper presents a sketch to an algorithm for mining and processing power tags in retrieval systems. Another study suggests developing a scheme for classifying web image queries via manual or automatic meta-tagging and one in which user queries can be employed as improved tools for image retrieval. The fourth sub-category *Taxonomy* tests a prototype for query taxonomy on image searches. The organization makes distinctions between general and specific queries, and points to general queries as the most frequent category. However, other studies indicate that a "down-top" approach shall be preferred and that specific objects and events taking place in the photograph are the most commonly used levels of description. Other findings conclude that search behavior is influenced by the query type and also depends on the user. The findings shed light on the importance of considering query categories to understand user behavior on image search platforms. Another focus is domain oriented, examining search facets for an image search system for creative professionals. Exploratory tests look at defining image similarity subjects. However, they do not have collective strategies of similarity assessment. Finally, one study considers the design recommendations that question whether the document-retrieval model that most search engines are based on (keywords go in, and a linear list of about 20 results come out) is appropriate. Research in the fifth sub-category, *User Needs,* focuses on the users and not so much on improvement of a system, and is largely based on tests. Abstract attributes are primarily used for search when users intend to use images as sources of objects, while specific attributes are explored when they use the images as sources of data. Images are often searched depending on the users' work, needs, and research areas, although images of particular maps and photographs are also searched for the users' own personal collections. Users prefer familiar web search engines to specialized image archives or databases. The results show that their appreciation can be sub-divided according to intended utilization whether it is work or research areas. Visual information seeking, however, is still in its infancy.

CHAPTER 3

Natural Scene Perception and Eye Tracking

Moving our eyes is a natural action and something we do not question in our daily life. Early in the development of medical science research there was an interest in understanding why and how eye movements happen. This led to research on how we use eye movements to understand the surroundings in which we are situated. Since the 1880s when the foundation of modern eye tracking technology is usually referred to (Wade and Tatler, 2005), a major research theme in eye tracking has been the relation between eye movement and the cognitive processes that can be identified when we are investigating our surroundings. This also includes the impact of visual stimuli on decision making (Jacob and Karn, 2003).

The research in eye movements is realized through various scientific fields, each with different research interests. Examples are given in psychology with the study of the link between cognition and eye movements, and in medicine where eye movements are studied as a manifestation of specific medical conditions. The use of eye movements as an input modality (or gaze interaction) where the eye movement is used as a substitute for mouse input is a research field that is attracting attention and with promising developments in the integration of eye tracking units in mobile devices.

The research on eye movements has led to the formulation of two main hypotheses. The so-called eye-mind hypothesis is based on the assumption that eye movements are controlled by the task we are participating in, which is the main driver of our visual attention. Consequently, eye movements are a result of top-down, high-level cognitive processes (Just and Carpenter, 1980). Other researchers have formulated a bottom-up hypothesis based on the assumption that eye movements are a result of intrinsic properties of the images that are exposed on our retina, thereby not involving higher levels of cognitive processes. Eye movements are driven by the hue and brightness of the image exposed, also known as the saliency of the image (Land and Tatler, 2009). In research, an integration of the two approaches is often used to explain the driving force behind eye movements. (ibid, 2009). The influence on the visual behavior of eye movements controlled by cognitive factors (top-down hypothesis) in the form of task activities was proven by Buswell (1935) and later by Yarbus (1967). Both authors offer vivid insight on how different tasks change how we inspect an image resulting in voluntary or guided eye movements. On the other hand, the bottom-up hypothesis based on involuntary eye movements is observed where our visual system responds to intrinsic features in an image, thereby guiding our gaze, i.e., color composition, dark or light objects, etc. This type of eye movement is also referred to as low-level eye control where the driving force behind eye movements is an unconscious activity and not the result of high-level cognitive factors (Holmqvist et al., 2011).

We move our eyeball because of the limitations set by the physiology of the eye. At the back of the eye is the fovea, the area with the highest visual acuity. Since the fovea is a relative small area, allowing for only a 2° movement, the eyeball has to be repositioned to gain the full color and light spectrum. We do have a peripheral view but what is projected at the borders of the fovea (outside the 2° field) is only recognized as a blurred black-and-white image. By eye movement we gain the full visual field of approximately 180°.

It is possible to divide eye movement into two main activities: saccadic eye movements and fixations. The saccadic eye movement is the actual repositioning of the eye resulting from a stimulus occurring in the surrounding world and demanding the repositioning of the eye to take place to obtain visual acuity. A saccadic eye movement is a very fast ballistic movement in the range of 30–40 ms and takes place approximately 3–4 times per second, depending on the changes in visual attention. It is generally assumed that we do not receive any visual input during a saccade in the form of a conscious visual input. A saccade is followed by a fixation considered as the time the eye is fixated upon an object and the visual input takes place. The actual fixation time is dependent on the visual stimulus we are observing and the task we are involved in. In reading tasks, fixation times from 202–264 ms have been reported (Rayner and Pollatsek, 1989) depending on type of literature. Henderson and Hollingworth (1999) report a fixation time of 330 ms in viewing pictures and natural scenes.

3.1   THE TECHNOLOGY BEHIND RECORDING EYE MOVEMENTS

To record eye movements an eye-tracking device or eye tracker is used. Eye trackers are available as remote eye trackers positioned in front of the user below a computer display or as a head-mounted eye tracker built into a pair of glasses. They each have their force and limitations. The advantage of a remote eye tracker is the known position relative to the image that is being studied. This facilitates easier calculations of the gaze coordinates but, on the other hand, limits the use of what can be displayed on the used display unit limited by factors such as screen size. A head-mounted eye tracker is not limited to what is displayed on a screen but can be used in a natural setting, allowing the user to move around freely. This allows for investigations of eye movements in settings such as a museum or studying how mobile devices are used. A limitation of head-mounted eye trackers can be the analysis of recorded data since the eye tracker is fixed on the person and not the scene being observed (see Holmqvist et al. (2011) for more technical details).

Figure 3.1: Test setup with remote eye tracker.

Figure 3.2: Remote eye tracker. Two infrared lights are seen below the screen. Eye camera(s) is positioned between light sources.

The eye tracker records eye movements using a video camera and a light source to create a reflection in the eye. The light source is usually emitting infrared (IR) light and illuminates the eye, creating a pupil and corneal reflection or glints. The video camera records an image of the eye-inclusive reflections, and the actual position or coordinate of the eye position is then calculated giving the gaze position of the eye. The sampling rate of commercial available eye trackers is usually in the range of 60–250 Hz, with specialized eye trackers achieving much higher sampling rates in the range of 1,000 Hz and higher. The recorded eye movements or gaze positions are often visualized as an overlay on the artifact observed (an image, a web page, movie, natural scene, etc.) showing the gaze path in the form of saccades and fixations. Evidently, it is also possible to access the actual recorded gaze coordinates for further analysis.

Figure 3.3: Modern eye tracking glasses with IR light and cameras built into frame.

3.2   EYE MOVEMENT RESEARCH

A number of research traditions have been established within the domain of eye movement since the foundation of modern eye movement research in the 1880s (Wade and Tatler, 2005). The research in eye movement includes research in the physiological construct of the eye and its inner workings, i.e., the muscular control of the eyeball, the function of the components of the eye, etc. This includes the function of the fovea and retina and the fact that we, with two eyes, are capable of a single vision. The other main area of research is related to our perceptual system, establishing hypotheses on what drives eye movements. The development of modern measuring techniques has driven this research since the 1880s, resulting in an ever-increasing use of eye movement research within a large number of disciplines, i.e., phycology, medicine, neuro medicine, etc. (Wade and Tatler, 2005). The technological development of measuring instruments and the minimization of the instruments, including a significant drop in the cost of high-quality instruments, has also resulted in the application of eye movement research in a setting that just a few years ago would have been considered impossible. This includes the development of portable equipment allowing for use outside dedicated research laboratories.

This wider use has also contributed to the establishment of well-documented experimental procedures and measurements.

Holmqvist et al. (2011) listed the four-main research traditions within eye movement research:

- research in visual search,

- research in text reading tasks,

- application of eye tracking in usability studies, and

- research in natural scene perception.

3.2.1   RESEARCH IN VISUAL SEARCH

Within each research tradition a number of theories have been developed to explain the drivers behind the eye movements that can be observed. This has also led to the definition of a number of measurements within each tradition. Visual search tasks and text reading tasks are probably the most researched within eye movement.

A visual search task is the situation where we have to find a specific thing or object among others. This includes activities such as locating a car key on a cluttered desk or icons on a computer screen. We can consider this an activity where the purpose is to identify a target among distractors. Visual search is probably the most common visual task we are involved in and two main activities have been identified. Parallel search is considered the activity taking place when the target object stands out against a number of distractors, like a blue object among red distractors. Even if the number of distractors is increased it is still fairly easy to identify the blue target object. Serial search takes place when the target object is difficult to distinguish from distractors, i.e., the shape of the target object does not stand out against distractors. In a parallel search task, the time to identify the target object is not influenced by an increase in the number of distractors, whereas serial search is characterized by an increase in search time for identifying a target object with an increase in distractors (Findlay and Gilchrist, 2003). According to Holmqvist et al. (2011), experimental procedures in visual search are easily adaptable and can inform us on how we cope with the rather large amount of visual information received by our eyes.

3.2.2   RESEARCH IN READING

The research in text reading is focused on text comprehension and the eye movements that can be identified in the process of reading. Research in text reading has been conducted at least since 1890 with the work of Javal (Findlay and Gilchrist, 2003). With the development of more advanced eye tracking equipment in the 1970s important research was done during the 1970s and 1980s in both the U.S. and Europe. This intensive research in text reading has led to the definition of important measurements as regressions as an expression of the difficulty of a text, i.e., more regressions by a user is considered as an expression of difficulties in understanding the actual text. This is also manifested in the actual reading speed measured in words per minutes (wpm). As reported by Rayner and Pollatsek (1989), considerable variation is seen between different types of text, ranging from 365 wpm in reading light fiction to texts from the domain of biology with 233 wpm. The number of regressions in percent follows the same pattern ranging from 5% in light fixtion to 18% in biology (ibid).

3.2.3   APPLICATION OF EYE TRACKING IN USABILITY STUDIES

A relatively new application of eye tracking has been within the area of usability research, where the use of eye tracking can be seen as a natural extension of existing data collection methods, providing added insights into the cognitive and behavioral aspects of the interaction between humans and machine. Eye tracking in the context of usability studies integrates research from the other main research traditions mentioned here.

3.2.4   NATURAL SCENE PERCEPTION

Research on eye movements in viewing images is positioned within the research tradition of natural scene perception. Natural scene perception deals with the activities involved in viewing and understanding visual scenes. This can be activities in a kitchen, looking at art in a museum, photographs, images presented on a computer screen, etc. A core research question in scene perception is: What are the drivers behind our oculomotor system to position the fovea in a specific position? As discussed previously, two main factors have been suggested for guiding our saccades toward a target: low-level features in the scene and high-level factors on a contextual or semantic level (Tatler and Vincent, 2008). The low-level cues or salience refers to features in a scene as luminance and edges. According to Tatler and Vincent (2008), a causal link between the distribution of low-level visual features and fixation cannot be established but they also underline that this does not exclude some sort of influence on eye movements from low-level visual information.

An important discussion with regard to low-level drivers of eye movements is also the influence of image composition on eye movements. In a literature review on the effect of pictorial balance in paintings on eye movements, Locher (1996) found that the perceptual, central region of a picture receives the first and most fixations and that this is different from the actual physical center of the image. The author also found that an observer provides few fixations on peripheral areas of an image. According to Locher, the actual image composition and the resultant decision by an observer on informative, pictorial elements is happening within the first very few fixations. It is also found that domain knowledge has an effect on the eye movements and numbers and length of fixations especially observed on abstract paintings. People knowledgeable about art show shorter and more focused fixations (relative to informative objects) than novices without any profound knowledge of art (ibid).

It was also found that, during the viewing time of a natural scene, changes in the numbers of fixations and length of saccades can be identified. The assumption is that long saccades and few fixations belong to—perhaps—an initial identification of important features in an image. This global scanning behavior is followed by shorter saccades and longer fixations on what is assumed to be local areas of images and driven by cognitive real-time processing, i.e., probably elements in the image that can be categorized as informative (Holmqvist et al., 2011). This was discovered earlier by Buswell (1935) who proposed that the early short fixations and long saccades of an image should be interpreted as an orienting phase followed by an in-depth inspection of informative objects in the image characterized by longer fixation and shorter saccades.

The high-level drivers of eye movements on a contextual and semantic level have been more strongly demonstrated by a number of researchers. The main hypothesis is that our eye movements are guided by the task we are undertaking and it has been shown that features (objects and regions) that do not contain information relevant for the given task are not looked at. Some of the first and also defining results have been provided by Buswell (1935) and Yarbus (1967).

Buswell did his research during the 1920s and 1930s and in his study from 1935 he presented the first accounts of eye scanning of images. He looked at how gaze path differs between individuals and found that after an initial phase where the scan paths are more or less equal, personal differences can be observed. He suggested that the rationale behind this is an initial common orientation of an image followed by an individual inspection of elements in an image according to what the observer finds informative in the images. Buswell also found that if people are given a specific task, i.e., look for a specific target in the image, this will drive the gaze pattern of the observer compared to situations where the observer is asked to look at a picture without any specific directions. Finally, Buswell also found that people with a background in art used shorter fixation times compared to art students.

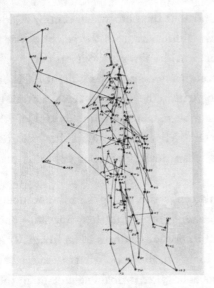

Figure 3.4: Gaze path of subject asked to look for a specific target object. From Buswell (1935, p. 138).

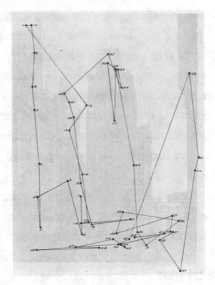

Figure 3.5: Gaze path of subject where no specific direction is given. From Buswell (1935, p. 137).

Probably one of the most cited experiments in viewing images is the experiment reported by Yarbus (1967), in which he described how people view complex objects, in this case "An Unexpected Visitor", a famous picture by Russian artist I. E. Repin. Yarbus presented 7 subjects with the same 7 tasks. Figure 3.6 shows the recordings of one observer's eye movement of the tasks which lasted for 3 min each. The first task was a free examination of the image whereas for tasks 2–7 the observer was given an instruction, i.e., for task 2 the instruction was to "Estimate the material circumstances of the family", task 3 was to "Give the ages of the people", etc.

In the free examination Yarbus found that participants tend to look at the faces of people present in the image followed by the bodies. Yarbus claims that the "Eye movements reflect the human thought process" (Yarbus, 1967, p. 190) and consequently the gaze path tells something about the participant's thoughts. Yarbus concludes that "The observer's attention is frequently drawn to elements which do not give important information but which, in his opinion, may so" (p. 191). In the tasks where a specific instruction was given, Yarbus found that the instruction had a profound impact on the eye movements of the observer and only objects in the image that contain information relevant for the task are viewed or at least attract the most fixations. This confirms the findings by Buswell.

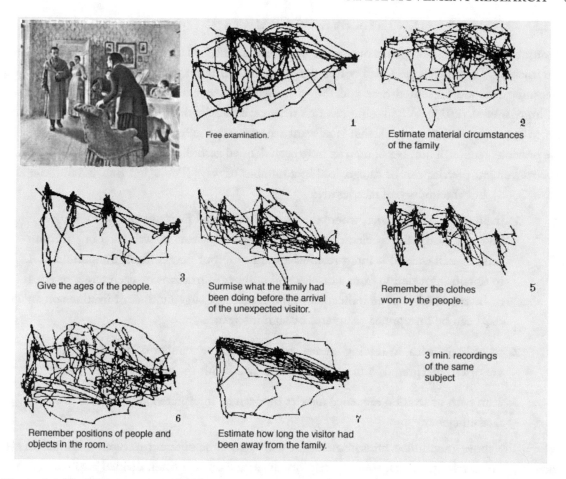

Free examination.   1

Estimate material circumstances
of the family   2

Give the ages of the people.   3

Surmise what the family had   4
been doing before the arrival
of the unexpected visitor.

Remember the clothes   5
worn by the people.

Remember positions of people and   6
objects in the room.

Estimate how long the visitor had   7
been away from the family.

3 min. recordings
of the same
subject

Figure 3.6: The Yarbus experiment. The task is driving eye movements. (Image from Wikipedia https://commons.wikimedia.org/wiki/File:Yarbus_The_Visitor.jpg)

Yarbus found that participants tend to demonstrate the same gaze pattern when given the same task even after a prolonged viewing time. Buswell, on the other hand, found a substantial difference in viewing pattern after an initial period where the gaze path showed a similarity between subjects. Yarbus acknowledged that during a relatively short time the observer obtains a general idea of the picture, but contrary to Buswell he observes that "Additional time spent on perception is not used to examine the secondary elements, but to reexamine the most important elements" (Yarbus, 1967 p. 193). And this is observed under a prolonged viewing time of more minutes. So according to Yarbus, people do not tend to differ in what they observe. Both Buswell and Yarbus observed that color has a very limited effect on scan path compared to black and white versions of the same image. This has also been verified by Tosi et al. (1997).

3.2.5   MEASUREMENTS IN EYE MOVEMENTS

A number of core measurements or metrics have been established since the foundation of modern eye tracking. The metrics are found within the research traditions mentioned above. A few selected measurements are presented here and for an in-depth presentation of eye tracking metrics see Holmqvist et al. (2011). When using research where eye tracking is applied, it is of course important to use an eye tracking metric that is relevant according to the activity studied. As mentioned in the previous section, a number of metrics have been defined according to task and cognitive activity. Eye movement metrics can be categorized in a number of ways (Poole and Ball, 2006; Jacob and Karn, 2003), but the important metrics are:

1. fixation-derived metrics, where the number of overall fixations can be indicative of how efficiently display elements are organized on a screen or website. Long fixation time overall (mean) is interpreted as an indication of how difficult the users find it to obtain information from a display and number of fixations on each target or Area of Interest (AOI) as an indication of importance. A large number of fixations on an AOI can be interpreted as an area of high interest;

2. saccadic metrics, in reading studies, for example, the number of regressive saccades are often interpreted as an indication of how difficult the text is to decode; and

3. scan path or fixation sequence metrics that can be interpreted as a measure of interface efficiency.

The above-mentioned measurements are used across the different research traditions in eye movement research. In natural scene perception, the actual scene is often divided into Areas of Interest (AOI) where each AOI identifies an object in the scene or a collection of objects. The division in AOIs is then used for calculating metrics as time to first fixation on AOI, number of fixations/fixation time on AOI, returning fixations to AOI, and distribution of the number of fixations/time on AOI. The saccade and fixation order within an AOI or between AOIs is also reported.

Eye trackers also record a number of other measures and besides the metrics mentioned above, pupil size and blink rate are often recorded and used as a measure of arousal and mental workload (pupil size) (Bojko, 2013) and cognitive load (blink rate) (Bentivoglio et al., 1997). These measures have found an application especially within the studies on the effects of advertisements and are combined with recording of eye movements.

3.2.6   RECENT DEVELOPMENTS

Not much has been published since 2005 on eye movements and image viewing. A study of academic papers in the databases of the Library and Information Science Abtract (LISA) and Library and Information Science & Technology Abstracts (LISTA) (Lund, 2016) reveals no papers on the relationship between eye movements and image tagging. A few articles, however, examine the relationship between existing tags, AOIs, and eye movements. Golbeck, Koepfler, and Emmerling (2011) performed a lab-based study intended to improve the understanding of the connection between social tags describing the content of an image and image tagging. Images are chosen because they are non-textual, and thus the content is not easily computer-manageable. The authors selected to work with images particularly from online art museum collections. Three researchers have identified AOIs in six images that were used as basic for the research questions with one about tagging behavior and the relationship to the number of AOIs in an image. Fifty-one subjects from social sciences, math/engineering/computer sciences, humanities, and physical science participated in the test where they tagged six images. Although this paper does not focus on eye-tracking data, AOIs prove useful as a method for comparing tagging behaviors across a wide variety of image types. The result also shows that there are significant differences in the number, order, and type of tags that users assign based on their experience with an image, the type of image tagged, and other image features.

Walber et al. (2012) studied the possibility of using the dwell-time on scene objects to indicate how important the object was based on the (longer) dwell time. The traditional way of manually assigning tags to images is in the number of circumstances no longer possible due to the explosion in the number of available images. Walber et al. claimed that a high number of tags provided by non-professionals on social media platforms like Flickr were not telling about the semantic structure of the image. Walber et al. therefore investigated the possibility of linking users' gaze pattern with image regions, thereby annotating images in a more detailed way and automatically assigning tags to objects. Walber et al. found that the users' gaze pattern allows for the identification of an image region with a precision of 67% when the user is shown a corresponding tag. If two regions are tagged, it is possible to differentiate the relevant regions with an accuracy of 38% (Walber et al. 2012, p. 11).

From the research in eye movements and natural scene perception the conclusion must be that the cognitive system tends to drive or guide the visual system according to the task a person is engaged in. This result in attention to features in a scene depending on a task where the object is considered to contain relevant information for the task-solving process is thoroughly inspected, whereas other elements not considered important are only briefly inspected. It is true that some low-level non-conscious activities are also taking place but it seems these are suppressed by higher-level task-driven activities.

3.3   EXPERIMENT

The general assumption in our experiment is that what we call free viewing of images cannot be characterized as a free viewing in the sense used by Buswell and Yarbus. In the experiment presented here, participants were asked to provide tags according to two different coding schemes. The coder was asked to describe the image according to different classes of information, i.e., time, place, etc. If we follow the findings by Buswell, Yarbus, and others, we must expect the coding scheme to influence the mental state of the coder. Employing the quote from Yarbus the eye movement is a result of human thought process and in case the user is presented with a specific task this will drive the eye movements accordingly.

To illustrate some of the arguments above we conducted a test of images where we asked the participants first to view a number of photographs with the task of tagging the images using two different coding schemes: Shatford's faceted classification (Shatford, 1986, Layne, 1994) and Ørnager's scheme for photographs (Ørnager, 1999). The actual tagging was done after the eye tracking session. Both schemes allow for tags describing abstract or associative elements in images as well as generic or real-life objects. This also includes time and place. For more details on the use of the schemes see Tables 3.1 and 3.2. The participants were informed before the test to tag the images for use in two newspapers, where one was a tabloid paper and the other an intellectual one. They were informed that the images were related to terror.

3.3.1   METHODOLOGY

Twelve undergraduate students following a course in image indexing were invited to participate in the study. Ten photographs were analyzed using a remote eye tracker device. Participants were informed about the scope of the test before the actual test. The eye tracking experiment was conducted in the usability facility at the Royal School of Library and Information Science in Copenhagen and the test participants and test moderators were present. Of the 12 test subjects, the recordings of 5 participants were not used in the data analysis due to a low quality in the eye tracking. In all, data from seven test subjects were deemed good. The experiment was conducted using a T120 remote eye tracker from Tobii Technologies with a sampling rate of 120 Hz. In the following, first the results of the tracking experiment are reported followed by a comparison with the results of the tagging experiment.

The examination of the test subjects' gaze path provides information about how the images have been examined by the participants. This might help in understanding the relationship between what the images express and the tags assigned by the participants. To illustrate this the gaze patterns of one person's assessment of two different images is presented here. For both images, the gaze patterns after 1 s of dwell time and 15 s of dwell time are shown.

Figure 3.7: Image 1 gaze path after 1 s dwell time. Red dots are fixations. Copyright by d@rkmarmotte (https://www.flickr.com/people/darkmarmotte/).

Figure 3.8: Image 2 gaze path after 15 s dwell time. Copyright by d@rkmarmotte (https://www.flickr.com/people/darkmarmotte/).

After 1 s of dwell time, the central part of image 1 (see Figure 3.7), a fixation at the face of the person (girl) is found. A more elaborate inspection of the features in the image is reached after 15 s (Figure 3.8). Faces and the bodies of persons are fixated including central objects in the image. Few fixations are seen on the surrounding areas. The mean number of fixations among all 7 test subjects is 2.57 after 1 s and 37.29 fixations after 15 s. Only 4 fixations among all test subjects are on the surrounding areas.

Figure 3.9: Image 2, gaze pattern after 1 s. Original photo: Hazem Bader, 2006, Image alteration: /anomalous https://www.flickr.com/photos/anomalous/2908478901/.

Figure 3.10: Image 2, gaze pattern after 15 s. Original photo: Hazem Bader, 2006, Image alteration: /anomalous https://www.flickr.com/photos/anomalous/2908478901/.

The gaze pattern on image 2 (Figure 3.9) follows the main object (gun) pointing directly at a person's head. As in image 1, the head of the person is fixated after 1 s. After 15 s dwell time, most of the fixations are seen in the upper half of the image (Figure 3.10), with fixations mainly on the head of the persons. After 1 s, the mean number of fixations is 4.57 and after 15 s it is 38.86 fixations. A majority of the fixations are on people in the image.

3.3.2 ANALYSIS OF ASSIGNED TAGS

As an example of the tags selected by the test subjects, the chosen tags for two images using Ørnager's groups (Ørnager, 1999) and Shatford's classes (Chung and Yoon, 2009) is displayed below.

Table 3.1: Ørnager's taxonomy with example of assigned tags. Image 1 and Image 2 refer to Figures 3.7 and 3.9

Ørnager Groups	Example: Tag Image 1	Example: Tag Image 2
A : Emotions and mood	Anxiety, evilness, fear,	Occupation, fear, threat
B : Associations	Child abuse, monster	Manipulation, power
C : Known persons		Soldier
D : Persons (anonymous)	Child, little girl	Boy, child, men
E : Real-life object	Ball, blood	Gun, scarf
F : Event		War, market
H : Geographic information	City, street, yard	Bazar, tunnel, Arab county
I : Time / time of year	day	day

Table 3.2: Shatford's taxonomy or classes with example of assigned tags. Image 1 and Image 2 refer to Figures 3.7 and 3.9

Shatford Classes	Example: Tag Image 1	Example: Tag Image 2
A: Abstract		
A1: Abstract object		
Mythical or fictitious	Monster	
A2: Emotion/abstract		
A2-1: Symbolic values	Horror	Conflict
A2-2: General feeling	Creepy	Afraid
A2-3: Individual affection, emotional cue	Crying, sadness	Fear, sadness
Emotion/Abstract	Anxiety, betrayal	Terror
A3: Abstract location		
A3: Place symbolized	Urban	Middle East

G: Generic		
G1: Generic object		
G1-1: Kind of person	Girl, police, man	Soldier
G1-2: Kind of animal		
G1-3: Kind of thing	Balloon, blood	Helmet
Generic object	Leaf	Rifle
G2: Generic event/object		
G2-1: Kind of event		War
G2-2: Kind of action	Kidnapping	
Generic event/activity		
G3: Generic location		
G3: Kind of place		Bazar, street, tunnel
G4: Generic time		
G4: Cyclical time	Summer	Day
S: Specific		
S1: Specific object		
S1	Man	
S3: Specific location		
Individually named geographic location	Middle East	Arab country

Comparing the tags provided in Tables 3.1 and 3.2 with the gaze pattern in Figures 3.7 and 3.9 provides a pattern reflecting the tagging of objects seen in the image. Not surprisingly, objects belonging to what Shatford classifies as "Generic Classes" are examined. Tags belonging to Shatford's abstract classes and Ørnager's "emotional" and "association" are difficult to decode from the eye movements of the test subjects since emotional response to the content of an image is not directly expressed in the gaze pattern. What is also seen from comparing the assigned tags to Image 1 and Image 2 with the gaze pattern is that the fixations on objects in the images are not necessarily reflected in the tags assigned. The majority of tags assigned to Image 1 can be categorized as expressing emotional features in the image, i.e., tags such as crying, sad, and sadness whereas only 2 tags describing actual or generic objects in the image are found, i.e., child and girl. The gaze pattern shows a much more in-depth examination of the image with fixations at a number of objects as reported above. The gaze pattern seen at Image 2 also reveals a thorough examination of the image, but as with Image 1 only a few objects fixated are actually reported with tags. Mostly generic tags are used, i.e., boy, soldier, and gun. Only war is used as an emotional tag. As for Image 1, the actual number of fixations is reported above.

An analysis of all tags assigned to all images (N=8) shows that with the use of Ørnager's coding scheme 644 tags are assigned. The smallest number of tags given by a test person is 33 with a maximum of 89. Most tags are of type generic. In the group of emotional tags 50% are duplicate tags (82 tags) and only 36% (172 tags) unique tags are used in the class generic (Table 3.3).

Test Subject #	All tags	Emotional (group A,B)	Generic
1	33	5	28
2	33	7	26
3	89	27	62
4	67	11	56
5	74	32	42
6	47	5	42
7	50	6	44
8	79	24	55
9	36	9	27
10	55	14	41
11	45	16	29
12	36	8	28
Sum	644	164	480
Minimum	33	5	26
Maximum	89	32	62
Median	48,5	10	41,5

Table 3.3: Number of tags assigned to all images by all participants following Ørnager's coding scheme

When using the coding scheme proposed by Shatford the same pattern as with Ørnager's coding scheme is seen. In all, 535 tags are assigned, and the majority of tags belong to the generic classes (78%), and 118 (22%) are of the abstract types. In the abstract classes 48% of the tags are unique, and in generic classes 40% of the tags are found as unique (Table 3.4).

Table 3.4: Number of tags assigned to all images by all participants following Shatford's coding scheme

Test Subject #	All tags	Abstract Classes	Generic Classes
1	35	5	30
2	28	5	23
3	55	12	43
4	55	8	47
5	61	28	33
6	47	3	44
7	33	5	28
8	48	14	34
9	38	9	29
10	52	9	43
11	46	14	32
12	37	6	31
Sum	535	118	417
Minimum	28	3	23
Maximum	61	28	47
Median	46,5	8,5	32,5

The test subjects were asked to consider tags relevant for indexing the images for use in a news media setting. It is therefore not surprising that the majority of tags describe generic features in the images, i.e., tags describing actual physical objects. The gaze pattern of the test subjects also reveals an in-depth inspection of the images.

With a task of providing tags to images for indexing, the expected gaze pattern is likely to reflect the objects in the images and result in a pattern that is similar to a free examination, according to Yarbus (1967). Yarbus found that test subjects asked to perform a free-viewing task of an image results in an exhaustive inspection of the image features. The conclusion could be that the test subject is searching for all relevant objects in the image. This does not necessarily mean that the viewed objects are tagged. As seen from the examples in Figures 3.7 and 3.9, the test subject observes substantially more objects than reflected in the tags assigned. One reason for this could be the instruction to the test subject asking them to consider the images as related to terror. This might lead to a refinement of tags assigned reflecting what the test person relates to the concept of terror. The literature study in Chapter 2 indicates a predisposition to prefer generic indexing terms, although some discrepancy can be observed. The results of this experiment demonstrate that the most-used terms are generic, regardless of the coding scheme applied. This confirms the findings presented in the discussion about Indexing (p. 55). It is important to notice that the experiment presented here is user tagging of photos without the use of a controlled vocabulary or a taxonomy. We therefore cannot conclude what the results would have been using a taxonomy as a tool for indexing, but, according to previous research, the use of controlled vocabulary terms with social tagging results in a better treatment of the photograph semantics (see p. 54). Looking at the participants' eye movement we see a comprehensive inspection of the photographs and the objects contained in the image. Compared to the findings from using the coding schemes presented above we see that objects belonging to the generic classes are observed. This could lead to the conclusion that, with appropriate algorithms for automatic object identification, an automated tagging of generic image objects could be achieved. Walber (2012) found that the dwell time length can tell us about the importance of objects in images but this still leaves us with the problem of translating this information into concepts belonging to the abstract classes in the coding schemes. What we can see is that not all objects gazed at are tagged. This could be interpreted as a selection process where the task given decides what objects should be tagged. But the main question is still—Can we tell anything about the image context without using human indexing?

CHAPTER 4

Trends in Handling Future Image Collections

The most significant purpose of research is to push boundaries, and the question is if any borders have moved since the onset of social media. The literature review and citation maps show that the traditional research areas on images now include crowdsourcing and tagging which are related to social media. However, the biggest change has been the advent of large image collections collected from social networks such as Flickr. These collections provide researchers with new testbeds for improving or testing research hypotheses on a scale not possible before. We are living in the digital era and technology and social networks truly affect us. We tend to believe that problems can be solved by technology alone, forgetting that a problem needs to be solved before utilizing technology. Therefore, as Mette Sandbye explains, "As of now, this enormous wealth of photographically documented, shared and archived everyday life is not reflected in the amount and depth of research done on this kind of material." We still need research about images even though technology is evolving.

What we do not witness is the adaption of any experience from academic image research to the private photos on social media. The motivation to provide metadata seems to be driven by personal benefit more than community benefit, i.e., supporting the individual's social presence. Research also finds that a majority of tags provided are tags describing persons or objects depicted and, to a lesser extent, tags describing abstract features. To support the tagging of photographs it seems that technology supporting point-of-capture tagging, e.g., on a mobile device, motivates users. The professional user or professional image collection uses image indexing within the scope of organizing the collection for future use, i.e., efficient support of image retrieval. This means the use of formalized indexing procedures including controlled vocabularies. With the introduction of crowdsourcing in professional collections, the strict adherence to well-established guidelines is challenged but seems to work as a valuable addition to professional indexing. The approach in research for analyzing image indexing and the categorization of tags is based on the work of Panofsky and Shatford. However, we do perceive experiments about various domains, indexing, and retrieval of images on social media and these experiments lead to new understanding.

Is there a future for photographic media?

Mette Sandbye

Indeed there is. Today photographs are produced and shared as never before, from private or semi-private amateur images of everyday life shared on all sorts of Internet platforms, to media images or so-called "stock" photography, collected and distributed by large, global photo agencies. I am sure that this explosive image growth will continue to an extent that we cannot even imagine today. The world is sensed as "visual" and people document their daily lives visually as never before. A lot of this visual material can be found on the Internet, but at the same time one could mention all kinds of photo archives at museums or all sorts of local institutions, booming with interesting visual archive material. This is a challenge for academic research: there is so much material to look into, relevant for anthropologists, historians, sociologists, art historians, you name them. As of now, this enormous wealth of photographically documented, shared, and archived everyday life is not reflected in the amount and depth of research done on this kind of material. Or, from a more critical angle, the implicit dangers of a monopolization of history and political events appears as a result of the concentration of photographs in large, commercial "pools", archives, or companies, could be addressed and analyzed much more by academia.

Cooperation between image taggers and academia by using crowdsourcing points to new ways of collaboration which may even have an effect on images on social media. The development of large training data for machine learning was done by Fei Fei (Savage, 2016) utilizing Amazon Mechanical Turk, which provided small payments to almost 50,000 people willing to hand-label nearly a billion images which can be found on image-net.org. Microsoft, at the same time, has developed the Common Objects in Context (COCO) dataset, which contains more than 300,000 images, each labeled with 5 captions (ibid). Another approach is the development of different guidelines or knowledge-sharing tools in image description. A blended mode can be used for indexing, as Springer et al. (2008) referred to in their report about users tagging historic photos already indexed by LC. Such broadminded guidelines can point to additional areas within different domains. Content description where researchers look at the query categories to understand user behavior on image search platforms is extensively studied and the same goes for retrieval models. Most search engines are based on the pattern where keywords go in and a linear list of about 20 results come out; however, the question is if this is appropriate or if other algorithms can substitute it. Before we can implement any changes to the algorithms, we need more research about humans' retrieval requirements.

We noted that the collaboration between information and computer science has intensified, and CBIR, which is derived from pattern recognition (e.g., fingerprints, x-rays, and face recognition) is but one example. Pattern recognition can be defined in several ways but one popular description is that it is a study of ideas and algorithms that provide computers with a perceptual capability to put abstract objects, or patterns, into categories in a simple and reliable way. In the academic image research literature it has specifically been utilized for automatic factual topics like color, shape, texture, etc. Technology, Entertainment, Design (TED) is a media organization which posts talks online for free distribution, under the slogan "ideas worth spreading". TED's early emphasis was technology and design but it has since broadened its focus to include talks on many scientific, cultural, and academic topics. According to one TED talk by Fei-Fei (2016), who is an Associate Professor of Computer Science and works in the areas of computer vision and cognitive neuroscience at Stanford University, "computers are roughly as good at describing the content of images as a three-year-old child." She says "The complete level, on par with an adult, college-degreed human, I think is going to be a long way off." So we cannot expect algorithms yet to display true visual intelligence, although the computer today does a better job clarifying the content of a photograph than it could a couple of years ago. One of the issues, when we consider object recognition, is the difficulties with different angles of an object or item. Fei-Fei takes the example of a cat where she explains that the template for Cat1 (Figure 4.01) is hard for the computer to equal to Cat2 (Figure 4.02) because the pattern is altered. It may require a new understanding and then the two templates have to refer to the same semantic expression CAT which involves text recognition. The computer has to be trained.

Figure 4.1: **Cat1** (Image-net.com).

Figure 4.2: **Cat2** (Image-net.com).

Computer programs can correctly detect people in a boat in a particular photo; however, if one asks what they are doing in the boat we are not at the point of understanding what is going on in that image (Savage, 2016). A human can effortlessly figure that out, but as images usually convey a multitude of meanings we are facing the challenge with polysemy. Rüger (2011, p. 172) claims that the "users who submit an image … could have a dozen different information needs in mind," however, "user feedback can change the weights of features in content-based retrieval scenarios." Richard Zemel, a computer scientist at the University of Toronto, is working on training the computer to answer arbitrary questions about an image, but the work is still in its early stages. He explains that "the currently available dataset is not large enough" (Ren, Kiros, and Zemel, 2015, p. 8) for the computer to learn. Based on Fei-Fei, Rüger, and Zemel's statements above, one can easily understand that it is still worth studying image indexing and retrieval, even though the prognoses state that in a few years photos may be read and analyzed by computers. If computers are to learn new ways of recognizing images, the researchers need to be at the forefront with image research. We believe that there are still many approaches that we as researchers/humans have to cover and that academia in various fields has not explored the potential of images yet. When it comes to social media, personal photos are used more and more as society becomes notably visual, but service providers have to rely on the research done in the field if they want to introduce new approaches, which has been endorsed. Still, as Louise Broch says in her interview, one has to think about the sentimental part, too, as many users are interested in the visual past. Therefore, more research in visual literacy may prove important and here the AAT, TGM, and LCSH thesauri may be utilized as backbone tools.

Is there a future for photographic media?
Louise Broch

Jokingly—I will say nostalgia, however, of course we are inclined to have the still photograph, although it is hard to find the images only based on technical metadata. It is a prerequisite to have a semantic description of the photograph in order to locate it. Regrettably, many historical images lack the semantic representation and in this case crowdsourcing turns out to be important for indexing and retrieval of the photograph.

Two major conferences are also concerned with digitalization, i.e., Special Interest Group on Computer GRAPHics and Interactive Techniques (SIGGRAPH) where most of the companies are in the engineering, graphics, motion picture, or video game industries, and Text REtrieval Conference (TREC), which is an ongoing series of workshops focusing on a list of different information retrieval (IR) research areas, or tracks. The latter encourages research within the information retrieval community. Although nothing explicit is about image research in LIS a lot of the experiments are important for this area.

Eye-tracking, as we have experimented with as an image evaluation tool and a device for additional tagging, is another renewed area where information and computer science work together. With an eye-tracking test, a person's interests can be mapped and read. However, as written in Chapter 3 about eye-tracking, both Buswell (1935) and later Yarbus (1967) find that if people are given a specific task, i.e., look at a specific target in the image, this will drive the gaze pattern of the observer compared to situations where the observer is asked to look at a picture without any specific directions. According to the research, the instruction had a profound impact on the eye movements of the observer, and only objects in the image that contain information relevant for the task are viewed or at least attract the most fixations. Our experiment with eye-tracking confirms the above claim that test persons are unsure about what to look for in images if they do not have a subject covering all the photos. However, we are inclined to encourage new surveys with eye-tracking testing, whether model pictures can be generated where preferred or favorite issues/topics are tagged and marked for searching in various domains.

The main problem in indexing and retrieval is that the emotional expressions are not yet solved, therefore we still face the questions about computers' visual abilities compared to the semantic understanding in the human brain. As Fei Fei (2016) put it, we have to focus on the amalgamation of the images and text corpus. In a study from 2010, SD and SAM were suggested as possible solutions. SD is a scale used for measuring the meaning of things and concepts and measuring connotative meaning, and SAM is an emotion assessment tool that uses graphic scales, depicting cartoon characters expressing three emotion elements: pleasure, arousal, and dominance. SAM seems, however, to be outdated while SD may be tried further in image research, especially regarding query categories, which can lead to lumps of emotional domain-dependent classes taking into account that nothing is stationary. However, Zemel (Ren, Kiros, and Zemel, 2015) insists that a larger database of questions and answers about images is required for the computer to learn.

Is there a future for photographic media?

Mette Kia Krabbe Meyer

When photography was invented futurologists said it was the death of painting. When film was invented, the same was said about photography. They were wrong. Photographs continued and continue to be taken. Ever-new ways of using photography in science, press, and private life develops as technology evolves and different spheres are merging. I have no reason to believe that this is not going to continue.

We are still trying to understand what photography means to us today in so many different contexts. Some researchers say that the photographic image in itself—when you look at amateur photography—is considered less and less interesting. What counts now, they say, is the photographic act or maybe even just the idea of taking a photograph. If people were overwhelmed by the sheer number of photographs they were seeing in the 1920s, today we are armed with cameras all the time and constantly in search of motives. A lot of people experience reality through a camera. Whether they actually take the photograph or even look at it afterwards is secondary. On an overall level we are taking and circulating a rising number of photographs within all kinds of professions and on social media.

Mette Kia Krabbe Meyer expresses, "Ever new ways of using photography in science, press and private life develops as technology evolves and different spheres are merging. I have no reason to believe that this is not going to continue." New areas may be expected in research and technology but the photography will continue to exist if we believe that the saying "a picture is worth a thousand words" still counts. Additionally, we have Fei Fei's word about computers not being able to decipher what is going on in an image (Savage, 2016). Her judgment points to a lot of new research in the image field paired with text recognition, and with computers evolving there is a great potential for more cooperation with computer science. We have outlined several topics based on the literature survey and our recent research in image eye-tracking, however, there are no limitations to what may be studied. We could not have imagined new research fields since the introduction of social networks, but even with the inaugurated surveys there are challenges facing whoever wants to dive into the image depths.

Bibliography

Albertson, D. (2015). Visual information seeking. *Journal of the American Society for Information Science and Technology*, 66(6), 1091–1105. DOI: 10.1002/asi.23244. 52, 53

Ames, M. and Naaman, M. (2007). Why we tag: Motivations for annotation in mobile and online media. *CHI 2007*, April 28–May 3, 2007, San Jose, CA, 1–10. DOI: 10.1145/1240624.1240772. 27, 28, 40

André, P., Cutrell, E., Tan, D. S., and Smith, G. (2009). Designing novel image search interfaces by understanding unique characteristics and usage. In Gross, T. et al. (Eds.). *Human-Computer Interaction – INTERACT 2009*, 340–353. *Lecture Notes in Computer Science*, vol. 5727. Springer, Berlin, Heidelberg. DOI: 10.1007/978-3-642-03658-3_40. 52, 53

Angus, E., Stuart, D., and Thelwall, M. (2010). Flickr's potential as an academic image resource: An exploratory study. *Journal of Librarianship and Information Science*, 42(4), 268–278. DOI: 10.1177/0961000610384656. 25, 27, 40

Armitage, L. H. and Enser, P. G. B. (1997). Analysis of user need in image archives. *Journal of Information Science*, 23(4), 287–299. DOI: 10.1177/016555159702300403. 16, 35

Baca, M., Harpring, P., Lanzi, E., McRae, L., and Whiteside. A. B. (2006). *Cataloging Cultural Objects: A Guide to Describing Cultural Works and Their Images (CCO)*. Chicago: American Library Association. 33, 34

Barthes, R. (1961). The photographic message. In Susan Sontag (Ed.), *A Barthes Reader* (194-210.). New York: Hill and Wang, 1994. 6, 8

Barthes, R. (1964). Rhetoric of the Image. In Heath, S. (Ed.) *Roland Barthes: Image – Music – Text*, London: Fontana Press, 1977. Originally published as "Rhétorique de l'image" in Communications 4: 40–51. DOI: 10.1007/978-1-349-03518-2. 4, 5, 8, 38

Barthes, R. (1969). *Mytologier [Mythologies]*. København, Rhodos. 5, 38

Barthes, R. (1980). Billedets retorik [The rhetoric of the image]. In Fausing, B., and Larsen, P. (Eds.), *Visuel Kommunikation [Visual Communication]*, bd. 1 (42–57). Copenhagen: Medusa, 1980. 5, 8, 38

Beaudoin, J. E. (2012). Context and its role in the digital preservation of cultural objects. *D-Lib Magazine*, 18(11/12). DOI: 10.1045/november2012-beaudoin1. 26, 27, 40

Beaudoin, J. E. (2014). A framework of image use among archaeologists, architects, art historians and artists. *Journal of Documentation*, 70(1), 119–147. DOI: 10.1108/JD-12-2012-0157. 21, 22

Beaudoin, J. E. (2015). Content-based image retrieval methods and professional image users. *Journal of the American Society for Information Science and Technology*, 67(2), 350–365, 2016. 45, 46

Beaudoin, J. E. (2016). Describing images: A case study of visual literacy among library and information science students. *College & Research Libraries*, 77(3), 376–392. DOI: 10.5860/crl.77.3.376. 34, 40

Benjamin, W. (2015). On Photography. Edited and translated by Esther Leslie. London: Reaktion Books. 5

Benson, A. C. (2011). Relationship analysis of image descriptions: An ontological, content analytic approach. Unpublished doctoral dissertation, University of Pittsburgh, Pennsylvania.

Benson, A. C. (2015). Image descriptions and their relational expressions: a review of the literature and the issues. *Journal of Documentation*, 71(1), 143–164. DOI: 10.1108/JD-07-2013-0093. 31, 32, 40

Bentivoglio, A. R., Bressman, S. B., Cassetta, E., Carretta, D., Tonali, P., and Albanese, A. (1997). Analysis of blink rate patterns in normal subjects. *Movement Disorders: Official Journal of the Movement Disorder Society*, 12(6), 1028–1034. DOI: 10.1002/mds.870120629. 70

Bojko, A. (2013). *Eye Tracking the User Experience: A Practical Guide to Research*. Brooklyn, NY: Rosenfeld Media. 70

Brinkman, S. and Kvale, S. (2015). *InterViews: Learning the Craft of Qualitative Research Interviewing*. 3rd ed. London: Sage. 41

Buhl, M. (2011). Billeder og visualiseringer i et fagligt tværgående didaktisk perspektiv. In: Krogh, E., and Nielsen, F. V. (Ed.), *Sammenlignende Fagdidaktik*, (97–118). Aarhus: Cursiv Danmark.

Burford, B., Briggs, P., and Eakins, J. P. (2003). A taxonomy of the image: on the classification of content for image retrieval. *Visual Communication*, 2(2), 123–161. DOI: 10.1177/1470357203002002001. 21

Buswell, G. T. (1935). *How People Look at Pictures: A Study of the Psychology and Perception in Art*. Chicago: University of Chicago Press. 61, 67, 68, 82

Chandler, D. (1994). *Semiotics for Beginners*. Available at: http://visual-memory.co.uk/daniel/Documents/S4B/ (accessed May 23, 2017).

Chandler, D. (2002). *Semiotics: The Basics*. London: Routledge. DOI: 10.4324/9780203166277. 4

Chen, H. (2001). An analysis of image queries in the field of art history. *Journal of the American Society for Information Science and Technology*, 52(3), 260–273. https://doi.org/10.1002/1532-2890(2000)9999:9999<::AID-ASI1606>3.0.CO;2-M. 16, 46

Chen, H., Kochtanek, T., Burns, C. S., and Shaw, R. (2010). Analyzing users' retrieval behaviors and image queries of a photojournalism image database. *The Canadian Journal of Information and Library Science*, 34(3), 249–270. DOI: 10.1353/ils.2010.0003. 21, 22

Choi, Y. (2013). Analysis of image search queries on the web: Query modification patterns and semantic attributes. *Journal of the American Society for Information Science and Technology*, 64(7), 1423–1441. DOI: 10.1002/asi.22831. 48, 49

Choi, Y. and Hsieh-Yee, I. (2010). Finding images in an online public access catalogue: Analysis of user queries, subject headings, and description notes. *The Canadian Journal of Information and Library Science* 34(3), 271–298. DOI: 10.1353/ils.2010.0004. 47, 49

Choi, Y. and Rasmussen, E. M. (2003). Searching for images: The analysis of users' queries for image retrieval in American history. *Journal of the Association for Information Science and Technology*, 54(6), 498–511. DOI: 10.1002/asi.10237. 16

Christensen, H. D. (2017). Rethinking image indexing? *Journal of the Association for Information Science and Technology*, 68(7), 1782–1785. DOI: 10.1002/asi.23812. 9

Chu, H. T. (2001). Research in image indexing and retrieval as reflected in the literature. *Journal of the American Society for Information Science and Technology*, 52(12), 1011–1018. DOI: 10.1002/asi.1153.

Chung, E. K. and Yoon, J. W. (2009). Categorical and specificity differences between user-supplied tags and search query terms for images. An analysis of Flickr tags and Web image search queries. *Information Research*, 14(3). 46, 47, 49, 74

Chung, E. K. and Yoon, J. W. (2011). Image needs in the context of image use: An exploratory study. *Journal of Information Science*, 37(2), 163–177. DOI: 10.1177/0165551511400951. 52 , 53

Conduit, N. and Rafferty, P. (2007). Constructing an image indexing template for The Children's Society. Users' queries and archivists' practice. *Journal of Documentation*, 63(6), 898–919. DOI: 10.1108/00220410710836411. 35, 37, 41

Cunningham, S. J. and Masoodian, M. (2006). *Looking for a Picture: An Analysis of Everyday Image Information Searching* (198). ACM Press. DOI: 10.1145/1141753.1141797. 16

Deacon, D., Pickering, M., Golding, P., and Murdock, G. (1999). *Researching Communications: A Practical Guide to Methods in Media and Cultural Analysis*. London: Arnold.

Drew, S. and Guillemin, M. (2014). From photographs to findings: visual meaning-making and interpretive engagement in the analysis of participant generated images. *Visual Studies*, 29(1), 54–67. DOI: 10.1080/1472586X.2014.862994. 28, 40

Enser, P. (2000). Visual image retrieval: seeking the alliance of concept-based and content-based paradigms. *Journal of Information Science*, 26(4), 199–210. DOI: 10.1177/0165551004233212. 16

Enser, P. G. B. (2008a). The evolution of visual information retrieval. *Journal of Information Science*, 34(4), 531–546. DOI: 10.1177/0165551508091013.

Enser, P. G. B. (2008b). Visual image retrieval. In Blaise Cronin (Ed.): *Annual Review of Information Science and Technology* 42. ASIS&T, 1-42. DOI: 10.1002/aris.2008.1440420108.

Enser, P. G. B. and McGregor, C. G. (1992). Analysis of visual information retrieval queries. Report on Project G16412 to the British Library Research and Development Department, British Library, London. 46

Enser, P. G. B., Sandom, C. J., and Lewis, P. H. (2005). Automatic annotation of images from the practitioner perspective. In Leow, W.-K. et al. (Eds.), *CIVR 2005*, LNCS 3568, 497–506. DOI: 10.1007/11526346_53. 24, 25, 40

Enser, P. G. B., Sandom, C. J., Hare, J. S., and Lewis, P. H. (2007). Facing the reality of semantic image retrieval. *Journal of Documentation*, 63(4), 465–481. DOI: 10.1108/00220410710758977. 42, 53

Estelle´s-Arolas, E. and Gonza´lez-Ladro´n-de-Guevara, F. (2012). Toward an integrated crowdsourcing definition. *Journal of Information Science* 38(2), 189–200. DOI: 10.1177/0165551512437638. 32, 33, 40

Fauzi, F. and Belkhatir, M. (2013). Multifaceted conceptual image indexing on the world wide web. *Information Processing and Management* 49, 420–440. DOI: 10.1016/j.ipm.2012.08.001. 26, 27, 40

Fauzi, F. and Belkhatir, M. (2014). Image understanding and the web: a state-of-the-art Review. *Journal of Intelligent Information Systems*, 43, 271–306. DOI: 10.1007/s10844-014-0323-6. 26, 27, 40

Fei-Fei, L. (2016). How we teach computers to understand pictures. TED Talk. Available at: https://www.youtube.com/watch?v=40riCqvRoMs (accessed September 20, 2017). 81, 83

Ferecatu, M., Boujemaa, N., and Crucianu, M. (2008). Semantic interactive image retrieval combining visual and conceptual content description. *Multimedia Systems* 13(5), 309–322. DOI: 10.1007/s00530-007-0094-9.

Fidel, R. (1997). The image retrieval task: implications for the design and evaluation of image databases. *New Review of Hypermedia and Multimedia*, 3(1), 181–199. DOI: 10.1080/13614569708914689. 16

Findlay, J. M. and Gilchrist, I. D. (2003). *Active Vision: The Psychology of Looking and Seeing*. Oxford ; New York: Oxford University Press. DOI: 10.1093/acprof:oso/9780198524793.001.0001. 65, 66

Glaser, B. (1992). *Basics of Grounded Theory Analysis*. Mill Valley, CA: Sociology Press. 16

Glaser, B. and Strauss, A. (1967). *The Discovery of Grounded Theory*. Chicago: Aldine. 16

Göker, A., Butterworth, R., MacFarlane. A., Ahmed, T. S., and Stumpf, S. (2016). Expeditions through image jungles. *Journal of Documentation*, 72(1), 5–23, DOI: 10.1108/JD-01-2014-0019. 50, 51

Golbeck, J., Koepfler, J., and Emmerling, B. (2011). An experimental study of social tagging behavior and image content. *Journal of the American Society for Information Science and Technology*, 62(9), 1750–1760. DOI: 10.1002/asi.21522. 71

Golder, S. A. and Huberman, B. A. (2006). Usage patterns of collaborative tagging systems. *Journal of Information Science*, 32(2), 198–208. DOI: 10.1177/0165551506062337. 16

Goodrum, A. and Spink, A. (2001). Image searching on the Excite Web search engine. *Information Processing & Management*, 37(2), 295–311. DOI: 10.1016/S0306-4573(00)00033-9. 16

Greenberg, G. (2017). Content and target in pictorial representation. Department of Philosophy, UCLA [DRAFT], 1-39.

Greisdorf, H. and O'Connor, B. (2002). Modelling what users see when they look at images: a cognitive Viewpoint. *Journal of Documentation*, 58(1), 6–29. DOI: 10.1108/00220410210425386.

Hajibayova, L. (2013). Basic-level categories: A review. *Journal of Information Science*, 39(5) 676–687. DOI: 10.1177/0165551513481443. 44

Harkema, C. and Avery. C. (2015). Milne en Masse: A case study in digitizing large image collections. *New Review of Academic Librarianship*, 21(2), 249-255. DOI: 10.1080/13614533.2015.1034806. 23, 40

Harpring, P. (2009). Subject access to art works: Using CCO/CDWA & vocabularies (educational material). Available at: http://www.getty.edu/research/tools/vocabularies/subject_access_for_art.pdf (Accessed Mai 29, 2017). 33, 34

Henderson, J. M. and Hollingworth, A. (1999). High-level scene perception. *Annual Review of Psychology*, 50(1), 243–271. DOI: 10.1146/annurev.psych.50.1.243. 62

Hidderley, R. and Rafferty, P. (1997). Democratic indexing: an approach to the retrieval of fiction. *Information Services and Use*, 17(2/3), 101-111. DOI: 10.3233/ISU-1997-172-304. 42

Hjørland, B. (2005). *Lifeboat for Knowledge Organisation*. [Danmarks Biblioteksskole]. Available at: http://iva.dk/bh/Lifeboat_KO/home.htm [accessed January 1, 2017].

Holmqvist, K., Nyström, M., Andersson, R., Dewhurst, R., Jarodzka, H., and van de Weijer, J. (2011). *Eye Tracking: A Comprehensive Guide to Methods and Measures*. Oxford, New York: Oxford University Press. 62, 65, 67, 70

Huang, H. and Jörgensen, C. (2013). Characterizing user tagging and co-occurring metadata in general and specialized metadata collections. *Journal of the American Society for Information Science and Technology*, 64(9), 1878–1889. DOI: 10.1002/asi.22891. 29, 30, 40

Huang, X., Soergel, D., and Klavans, J. L. (2015). Modeling and analyzing the topicality of art images. *Journal of the American Society for Information Science and Technology*, 66(8), 1616–1644. DOI: 10.1002/asi.23281.

Hung, T. Y. (2005). Search moves and tactics for image retrieval in the field of journalism: A pilot study. *Journal of Educational Media and Library Sciences*, 42(3), 329–346.

Hung, T. Y. (2012). An analysis of photo editors' query formulations for image retrieval. *Journal of Librarianship and Information Studies*, 4(1), 13–16. 48, 49

Ingwersen, P. (1992). *Information Retrieval Interaction*. London: Taylor Graham. 53

Ingwersen, P. and Järvelin, K. (2005). *The Turn: Integration of Information Seeking and Retrieval in Context*. Dordrecht, NL: Springer. 53

IPTC Subject Codes (2017). Available at: https://iptc.org/standards/subject-codes/ (accessed May 15, 2017). 50

ISO (2009) ISO 15836:2009. Information and documentation—The Dublin Core Metadata Element Set. Available at: https://www.iso.org/standard/52142.html (accessed May 4, 2017). 30

Jacob, R. J. and Karn, K. S. (2003). Eye tracking in human-computer interaction and usability research: Ready to deliver the promises. *Mind*, 2(3), 4. DOI: 10.1016/B978-044451020-4/50031-1. 61, 70

Jansen, B. J. (2008). Searching for digital images on the web. *Journal of Documentation*, 64(1), 81 – 101. Permanent link to this document: http://dx.doi.org/10.1108/00220410810844169. 46, 49, 50

Jörgensen, C. (1995). Image attributes: An investigation (Indexing systems, retrieval systems, computerized). Unpublished doctoral dissertation, Syracuse University, NY. 21

Jörgensen, C. (1998). Attributes of images in describing tasks. *Information Processing and Management*, 34(2/3), 161–174. DOI: 10.1016/S0306-4573(97)00077-0. 46

Jörgensen, C. (2003). *Image Retrieval: Theory and Research*. Lanham, MA. Oxford:The Scarecrow Press.

Jörgensen, C. (2007). Image access, the semantic gap, and social tagging as a paradigm shift. *18th Annual ASIS SIG/CR Classification Research Workshop*, 1-9, DOI: 10.7152/acro. v18i1.12868. 24, 25, 40

Jörgensen, C. (2010). Still image indexing. *Encyclopedia of Library and Information Sciences*. 3rd ed. DOI: 10.1081/E-ELIS3-120044380.

Jörgensen, C. and Jörgensen, P. (2003). Image querying by image professionals. ASIST 2003. *Proceedings of the 66th ASIST Annual Meeting* (pp. 349–356). Medford, NJ: Information Today. DOI: 10.1002/meet.1450400143.

Jörgensen, C. and Jörgensen, P. (2005). Image querying by image professionals. *Journal of the American Society for Information Science and Technology*, 56(12), 1346–1359. https://doi.org/10.1002/asi.20229.

Jörgensen, C., Stvilia, B., and Wu, S. (2013). Assessing the relationships among tag syntax, semantics, and perceived usefulness. *Journal of the American Society for Information Science and Technology*, 65(4), 836–849, 2014. 29, 30, 40

Just, M. A. and Carpenter, P. A. (1980). A theory of reading: from eye fixations to comprehension. *Psychological Review*, 87(4), 329. DOI: 10.1037/0033-295X.87.4.329. 61

Kandiuk, M., Lupton, A., and Davidson, C. (2013). *Digital Image Collections and Services*. SPEC Kit 335. Washington DC:Association of Research Libraries. DOI: 10.29242/spec.335.

Klavans, J. L., LaPlante, R., and Golbeck, J. (2014). Subject matter categorization of tags applied to digital images from art museums. *Journal of the American Society for Information Science and Technology*, 65(1), 3–12. DOI: 10.1002/asi.22950.

Klenczon, W. and Rygiel, P. (2014). Librarian cornered by images, or how to index visual resources. *Cataloging & Classification Quarterly*, 52(1), 42–61. DOI:10.1080/01639374.2013.848123. 33, 34, 40

Knautz, K. (2012). Emotion felt and depicted: Consequences for multimedia retrieval. In Rasmussen Neal, D. (Ed.), *Indexing and Retrieval of Non-Text Information* (Chapter 14, pp. 343–375). Series: Knowledge and Information. Boston: De Gruyter Saur USA.

Konkova, E., Goker, A. S., Butterworth, R., and MacFarlane, A. (2014). Social tagging: Exploring the image, the tags, and the game. *Knowledge Organization*, 41(1), 57-65. 36, 37, 41

Konkova, E., MacFarlane, A., and Göker, A. (2016). Analysing creative image search information needs. *Knowledge Organization*, 43(1). 51

Kovács, B. L. and Takács, M. (2014). New search method in digital library image collections: A theoretical inquiry. *Journal of Librarianship and Information Science*, 46(3), 217–225. DOI: 10.1177/0961000614526611. 30, 40

Kracauer, S. (1927). *Photographie*. Translated by Thomas Y. Levin in *Critical Inquiry* 1993, 19(3), 421–436. 5

Lancaster, F. W. (2003). *Indexing and Abstracting in Theory and Practice*. London: Facet Publishing, Britain. 20, 49

Land, M. F. and Tatler, B. W. (2009). *Looking and Acting: Vision and Eye Movements in Natural Behavior*. Oxford, New York: Oxford University Press. DOI: 10.1093/acprof: oso/9780198570943.001.0001. 61

Larson, J. and Sandbye, M. (2014). *Digital Snaps: The New Face of Photography*. I. B. Tauris. 4

Layne, S. S. (1994). Some issues in the indexing of images. *Journal of the American Society for Information Science*, 4(8), 583–588. DOI: 10.1002/(SICI)1097-4571(199409)45:8<583::AID-ASI13>3.0.CO;2-N. 8, 30, 56, 72

Lee, H. J. and Neal, D. (2007). Toward web 2.0 music information retrieval: Utilizing emotion-based, user-assigned descriptors. *Proceedings of the Association for Information Science and Technology*, 44(1), 1–34. DOI: 10.1002/meet.1450440391. 38

Lee, H. J. and Neal, D. (2010). A new model for semantic photograph description combining basic levels and user-assigned descriptors. *Journal of Information Science*, 36(5), 547–565. DOI: 10.1177/0165551510374930. 49, 51

Leung, C. H. C., Li, Y., and Chan, W. S. (2013). Knowledge-based semantic retrieval of multimedia and image objects using collaborative indexing. *International Journal of E-Business Development*, 3(4), 179–188.

Lin, Y. L., Trattner, C., Brusilovsky, P., and He, D. (2015). The impact of image descriptions on user tagging behavior: A study of the nature and functionality of crowdsourced tags. *Journal of the American Society for Information Science and Technology*, 66(9), 1785–1798. DOI: 10.1002/asi.23292. 32, 33, 40

Locher, P. J. (1996). The contribution of eye-movement research to an understanding of the nature of pictorial balance perception: A review of the literature. *Empirical Studies of the Arts*, 14(2), 143–163. DOI: 10.2190/D77M-3NU4-DQ88-H1QG. 67

Lund, H. (2016). Eye tracking in library and information science: a literature review. *Library Hi Tech*, 34(4), 585–614. DOI: 10.1108/LHT-07-2016-0085. 38, 71

Maniu, S., O'Hare, N., Aiello, L. M., Chiarandini, L., and Jaimes, A. (2013). Search behavior on photo sharing platforms, presented at *IEEE International Conference on Multimedia and Expo* (*ICME*), July 15–19, 2013, San Jose, CA. DOI: 10.1109/ICME.2013.6607496. 50, 51

Markey, K. (1983). Computer assisted construction of a thematic catalog of primary and secondary subject matter. *Visual Resources*, 3(1), 16–49. DOI: 10.1080/01973762.1983.9659063. 7

Markula, M. and Sormunen, E. (n.d.). End-user searching challenges indexing practices in the digital newspaper photo archive. *Information Retrieval*, 1(4), 259–285. 16

Marshakova, I. (1973). System of documentation connections based on references (SCI). *Nauch-no-Tekhnicheskaya Informatsiya Seriya*, 2(6), 3–8. 13

Matusiak, K. K. (2013). Image and multimedia resources in an academic environment: A qualitative study of students' experiences and literacy practices. *Journal of the American Society for Information Science and Technology*, 64(8), 1577–1589. DOI: 10.1002/asi.22870. 36, 37, 41

McCain, K. W. (1991). Mapping economics through the journal literature: An experiment in journal cocitation analysis. *Journal of the American Society for Information Science*, 42(4), 290. DOI: 10.1002/(SICI)1097-4571(199105)42:4<290::AID-ASI5>3.0.CO;2-9. 13

The MIRFLICKR Retrieval Evaluation (2015). http://press.liacs.nl/mirflickr/ (accessed May 15, 2017).

Mehring, C. (1997). Siegfried Kracauer's theories of photography: From Weimar to New York. *History of Photography*, 21(2), 129–136, DOI: 10.1080/03087298.1997.10443730. 5

Mitchell, W. T. J. (1986). *Iconology. Image, Text, Ideology*. Chicago: University of Chicago Press.

Moher, D., Liberati, A., Tetzlaff, J., and Altman, D.G. (2009). Preferred reporting items for systematic reviews and meta-analyses: the PRISMA statement, *Annals of Internal Medicine*, 151(4), 264–269. 11

Mounika, B., Sowmya, Y., Pasala, S., and Sravani, A. (2016). Content-based image retrieval using color. *International Journal of Applied Engineering Research*, 11(6), 4331–4334. 46, 47

Nakatsu, R. T., Grossman, E. B., and Iacovou, C. L. (2014). A taxonomy of crowdsourcing based on task complexity. *Journal of Librarianship and Information Science*, 40(6), 823–834. DOI: 10.1177/0165551514550140. 32, 33, 40

Nations, D. (2017). *What Is Social Media? Explaining the Big Trend.* https://www.lifewire.com/what-is-social-media-explaining-the-big-trend-3486616. 1

Neal, D. (2008). News photographers, librarians, tags, and controlled vocabularies: Balancing the forces. *Journal of Library Metadata*, 8(3), 199–219. DOI: 10.1080/19386380802373936. 20, 21, 22

Neal, D. (2010). Emotion-based tags in photographic documents: The interplay of text, image, and social influence. *The Canadian Journal of Information and Library Science* 34(3), 329-353. DOI: 10.1353/ils.2010.0000. 38, 39, 41

Norbert, W. (1948). *Cybernetics: Or Control and Communication in the Animal and the Machine*. 2nd rev. ed. 1961. Paris: Hermann & Cie; Cambridge, MA: MIT Press.

Nov, O. and Ye, C. (2010). Why do people tag? Motivations for photo tagging. *Communications of the ACM*, 53(7), 128-131. DOI: 10.1145/1785414.1785450. 27, 28, 40

Obar, J. and Wildman, S. (2015). Social media definition and the governance challenge: An introduction to the special issue. *Telecommunications Policy*, 39(9), 745–750. DOI: 10.1016/j.telpol.2015.07.014. 1, 35

O'Connor, B. C. and Wyatt, R. B. (2004). *Photo Provocations: Thinking in, with, and about Photographs*. Lanham, MD, Oxford: Scarecrow Press. 44

Ørnager, S. (1992). The Image as an information resource. In: *Proceedings from the 8th Nordic Conference on Information and Documentation*, May 19-21, 1992, Helsingborg. Stockholm, Tekniska Litteraturrsällskapet, 17–21.

Ørnager, S. (1997). Image retrieval: Theoretical analysis and empirical user studies on accessing information in images. *Proceedings of the American Society for Information Science Annual Meeting* 34: 202–11. 5, 7, 8

Ørnager, S. (1999). Billeder og ord. Analyser, beskrivelse og –søgning af pressefoto (Images and words: Analyzes, Indexing and retrieveal of journalistic photos). Unpublished Doctoral dissertation, Institut for Computer Lingvistik, CBS, Copenhagen. 72, 74

Panofsky, E. (1939). Studies in iconology: Humanistic themes. In *The Art of the Renaissance*. S.l.: Oxford University Press, 1939. Reprint, New York: Harper Torchbooks, 1962. 33, 34

Panofsky, E. (1962). *Studies in Iconology: Humanistic Themes in the Art of Renaissance*. Reprinted, New York: Harper and Row. 7, 8

Panofsky, E. (1977). *Meaning in the Visual Arts*. London: Peregrine (originally published in 1955).

Park, J. Y., O'Hare, N., Schifanella, R., Jaimes, A., and Chung, C. W. (2015). A large-scale study of user image search behavior on the Web. Presented at *CHI 2015, Crossings*, April 18–23, 2015, Seoul, Korea, 985–994. DOI: 10.1145/2702123.2702527. 49, 50

Petek, M. (2012). Comparing user-generated and librarian-generated metadata on digital images. *OCLC Systems & Services: International Digital Library Perspectives*, 28(2), 101–111. DOI: 10.1108/10650751211236659. 27, 28, 31, 40

Peters, I. and Stock, W. G. (2010). Power tags in information retrieval, *Library Hi Tech*, 28(1), 81–93. Permanent link to this document: http://dx.doi.org/10.1108/07378831011026706. 47, 48, 49

Piras, L. and Giacinto, G. (2017). Information fusion in content based image retrieval: A comprehensive overview. *Information Fusion*, 37, 50–60. DOI: 10.1016/j.inffus.2017.01.003. 37, 41

Poole, A. and Ball, L. J. (2006). Eye tracking in HCI and usability research. *Encyclopedia of Human Computer Interaction*, 1, 211–219. DOI: 10.4018/978-1-59140-562-7.ch034. 70

Rafferty, P. and Albinfalah, F. (2014). A tale of two images: the quest to create a story-based image indexing system. *Journal of Documentation*, 70(4), 605-621. DOI: 10.1108/JD-10-2012-0130. 33, 34, 40

Rafferty, P. and Hidderley, R. (2007). Flickr and democratic indexing: Dialogic approaches to indexing. *Aslib Proceedings: New Information Perspectives*, 59(4/5), 397–410. DOI: 10.1108/00012530710817591. 25, 27, 40, 42, 51

Ransom, N. and Rafferty, P. (2011). Facets of user-assigned tags and their effectiveness in image retrieval. *Journal of Documentation*, 67(6), 1038–1066. http://dx.doi.org/10.1108/00220411111183582. 28, 30, 40

Rasmussen, E. M. (1997). Indexing images. *Annual Review of Information Science and Technology (ARIST)*, 32, 169–96. 16

Rayner, K. and Pollatsek, A. (1989). *The Psychology of Reading*. Englewood Cliffs, NJ: Prentice-Hall. 62, 66

Reichle, E. D., Pollatsek, A., Fisher, D. L., and Rayner, K. (1998). Toward a model of eye movement control in reading. *Psychological Review*, 105(1), 125. DOI: 10.1037/0033-295X.105.1.125.

Reilly, M. and Thompson, S. (2014). Understanding ultimate use data and its implication for digital library management: A Case Study. *Journal of Web Librarianship*, 8(2), 196-213. DOI: 10.1080/19322909.2014.901211. 52, 53

Ren, M., Kiros, R., and Zemel, R.S. (2015). Exploring models and data for image question answering. In proceedings *Advances in neural information processing systems 28: Annual Conference on Neural Information Processing Systems 2015*, December 7–12, Montreal, Qubec, Canada, 2953–2961. 82, 83

Rorissa, A. (2008). User-generated descriptions of individual images versus labels of groups of images: A comparison using basic level theory. *Information Processing and Management* 44, 1741–1753. DOI: 10.1016/j.ipm.2008.03.004. 15, 43, 44

Rorissa, A. (2010). A comparative study of Flickr tags and index terms in a general image collection. *Journal of the American Society for Information Science and Technology*, 61(11), 2230–2242. DOI: 10.1002/asi.21401. 35, 37, 41

Rorissa, A., Clough, P., and Deselaers, T. (2008). Exploring the relationship between feature and perceptual visual spaces. *Journal of the American Society for Information Science and Technology*, 59(5), 770–784. DOI: 10.1002/asi.20792. 15

Rorissa, A. and Iyer, H. (2008). Theories of cognition and image categorization: What category labels reveal about basic level theory. *Journal of the American Society for Information Science and Technology*, 59(7), 1–10. DOI: 10.1002/asi.20825. 44, 47, 54

Rosch, E., Mervis, C. B., Gray, W., Johnson, D., and Boyes-Braem, P. (1976). Basic objects in natural categories. *Cognitive Psychology*, 8(3), 382–439. DOI: 10.1016/0010-0285(76)90013-X. 15, 30, 42, 56

Rose, G. (2007). *Visual Methodologies. An Introduction to the Interpretation of Visual Materials* (2nd ed.). London: SAGE Publications Ltd.

Rüger, S. (2011). Multimedia resource discovery. In: Melucci M., Baeza-Yates R. (eds) *Advanced Topics in Information Retrieval*. 157–186. The Information Retrieval Series, vol 33. Berlin, Heidelberg: Springer. 81

Rui, Y., Huang, T. S., and Chang, S. F. (1999). Image retrieval: Current techniques, promising directions, and open issues. *Journal of Visual Communication and Image Representation* 10, 39–62. DOI: 10:1006/jvci.1999.0413. 31

Savage, N. (2016). Seeing more clearly. *Communications of the ACM*, 59(1), 20–22. DOI: 10.1145/2843532. DOI: 10.1145/2843532. 80, 81, 84

Sawant, N., Li, J., and Wang, J. Z. (2011). Automatic image semantic interpretation using social action and tagging data. *Multimedia Tools and Applications*, 51, 213–246. DOI: 10.1007/s11042-010-0650-8.

Schmidt, S. and Stock, W. G. (2009). Collective indexing of emotions in images. A study in emotional information retrieval. *Journal of the American Society for Information Science and Technology*, 60(5), 863–876. DOI: 10.1002/asi.21043. 38, 39, 41

Search Engine Watch (2016). 23 up-to-date stats and facts about Instagram you need to know. Retrived from https://searchenginewatch.com/2016/04/20/23-stats-and-facts-about-instagram/. xiii

Shannon, C. E. (1948). A mathematical theory of communication. *Bell System Technical Journal* 27(July): 379–423; (October): 623–656. 30

Shatford, S. (1986). Analyzing the subject of a picture: A theoretical approach. *Cataloguing and Classification Quaterly*, 6(3), 39–62. DOI: 10.1300/J104v06n03_04. 7, 8, 15, 16, 30, 56, 72

Small, H. (1973). Co-citation in the scientific literature: A new measure of the relationship between two documents. *Journal of the Association for Information Science and Technology*, 24(4), 265–269. DOI: 10.1002/asi.4630240406. 13

Small, H. and Griffith, B. C. (1974). The structure of scientific literatures I: Identifying and graphing specialties. *Science Studies*, 4(1), 17–40. DOI: 10.1177/030631277400400102. 13

Smeulders, A. W. M., Worring, M., Santini, S., Gupta, A., and Jain, R. (2000). Content-based image retrieval at the end of the early years. *IEEE Transactions on Pattern Analysis and Machine Intelligence*, 22(12), 1349–1380. DOI: 10.1109/34.895972. 16

Smith, M. K. (2006). Viewer tagging in art museums: Comparisons to concepts and vocabularies of art museum visitors. *17th Annual ASIS&T SIG/CR Classification Research Workshop*, 1-19. DOI: 10.7152/acro.v17i1.12492.

Springer, M., Dulabahn, B., Michel, P., Natanson, B., Reser, D., Woodward, D., and Zinkham, H. (2008). *For the Common Good: The Library of Congress Flickr Pilot Project*. Library of Congress, Washington. 18, 29, 35, 38, 56, 80

Stewart, B. (2010). Getting the picture: An exploratory study of current indexing practices in providing subject access to historic photographs. *The Canadian Journal of Information and Library Science* 34(3), 297–327. DOI: 10.1353/ils.2010.0005. 9, 18, 19, 20, 22

Stewart, B. (2013). Pictures in words: Indexing, folksonomy and representation of subject content in historic photographs. Doctoral dissertation, Edith Cowan University, Perth, Western Australia.

Stewart, B. (2015). Pictures into words. *The Indexer*, 33(1), 8–25. 19, 20, 22, 38

Strauss, A. and Corbin, J. (1990). *Basics of Qualitative Research. Grounded Theory Procedures and Techniques*. Newbury Park, CA: Sage. 16

Strauss, A. and Corbin, J. (1998). *Basics of Qualitative Research Techniques and Procedures for Developing Grounded Theory*, (2nd ed.). Sage Publications: London. 16

Stvilia, B. and Jörgensen, C. (2009). User-generated collection-level metadata in an online photo-sharing system. *Library & Information Science Research*, 31, 54–65. DOI: 10.1016/j.lisr.2008.06.006. 25, 27, 40

Stvilia, B. and Jörgensen, C. (2010). Member activities and quality of tags in a collection of historical photographs in Flickr. *Journal of the American Society for Information Science and Technology*, 61(12), 2477–2489. DOI: 10.1002/asi.21432. 31, 32, 40

Stvilia, B., Jörgensen, C., and Wu, S. (2012). Establishing the value of socially-created metadata to image indexing. *Library & Information Science Research*, 34, 99–109. DOI: 10.1016/j. lisr.2011.07.011. 29, 31, 32, 40

Tang, L. and Carter, J. A. (2011). Communicating image content. *Proceedings of the Human Factors and Ergonomics Society 55th Annual Meeting*. DOI: 10.1177/1071181311551102. 36, 37, 41

Tatler, B. W. and Vincent, B. T. (2008). Systematic tendencies in scene viewing. *Journal of Eye Movement Research*, 2(2). Retrieved from https://bop.unibe.ch/index.php/JEMR/article/view/2263. 66

Terras, M. (2011). The digital wunderkammer: Flickr as a platform for amateur cultural and heritage content. *Library Trends*, 59(4), 686–706. DOI: 10.1353/lib.2011.0022. 29, 30, 40

Terras, M. (2012). Image processing in the digital humanities. In Warwick, C., Terras, M., and Nyhan, J. (Eds.). *Digital Humanities in Practice* (Chapter 4, pp. 71-90). London: Facet Publishing Britain.

Tirilly, P., Huang, C., Jeong, W., Mu, X., Xie, I., and Zhang, J. (2012). Image similarity as assessed by users: A quantitative study, presented at *ASIST 2012*, October 26–31, 2012, Baltimore, MD. DOI: 10.1002/meet.14504901180. 50, 51

Tosi, V., Mecacci, L., and Pasquali, E. (1997). Scanning eye movements made when viewing film: Preliminary observations. *International Journal of Neuroscience*, 92(1–2), 47–52. DOI: 10.3109/00207459708986388. 69

Tousch, A. M., Herbin, S., and Audibert, J. Y. (2011). Semantic hierarchies for image annotation: A survey. *Pattern Recognition*, 45(2012), 333–345.

Ulloa, L. C., Mora, M. C. M., Pros, R. C., and Tarrida, A. C. (2015). News photography for Facebook: effects of images on the visual behavior of readers in three simulated newspaper formats. *Information Research*, 20(1).

Van Eck, N. J. and Waltman, L. (2014). Visualizing bibliometric networks. In Ding, Y., Rousseau, R., and Wolfram, D. (Eds.), *Measuring Scholarly Impact* (pp. 285–320). Cham: Springer International Publishing. DOI: 10.1007/978-3-319-10377-8_13. 12, 13

Van House, N. A. (2007). Flickr and public image-sharing: Distant closeness and photo exhibition. *CHI 2007, Work-in-Progress*, April 28–May 3, 2007, San Jose, CA, 1–6. DOI: 10.1145/1240866.1241068.

Vander Wal, T. (2005). Explaining and showing broad and narrow folksonomies. Available at: www.vanderwal.net/random/entrysel.php?blog=1635 (accessed May 15, 2017). 47, 54

Wade, N. J. and Tatler, B. W. (2005). *The Moving Tablet of the Eye: The Origins of Modern Eye Movement Research*. Oxford, New York: Oxford University Press. DOI: 10.1093/acprof:oso/9780198566175.001.0001. 61, 64, 65

Walber, T., Scherp, A., and Staab, S. (2012). Identifying objects in images from analyzing the users' gaze movements for provided tags. Advances in Multimedia Modeling. *18th International Conference, MMM 2012*, Klagenfurt, Austria, January 4–6, 2012. Proceedings. 138–148. DOI: 10.1007/978-3-642-27355-1_15. 71, 78

Walsh, I., Holton, J. A., Bailyn, L., Fernandez, W., Levina, N., and Glaser, B. (2015). What grounded theory is …A critically reflective conversation among scholars. *Organizational Research Methods*, 18(4), 581–599. DOI: 10.1177/1094428114565028. 16

Westman, S. and Oittinen, P. (2006). Image Retrieval by End-users and Intermediaries in a Journalistic Work Context. *Information Interaction in Context: International Symposium on Information Interaction in Context*: IiiX : Copenhagen, Denmark, October 18–20, 2006, 102–110. DOI: 10.1145/1164820.1164843. 20, 21, 22

White, H. D. and Griffith, B. C. (1981). Author cocitation: A literature measure of intellectual structure. *Journal of the Association for Information Science and Technology*, 32(3), 163–171. DOI: 10.1002/asi.4630320302. 13

White, H. D. and McCain, K. W. (1998). Visualizing a discipline: An author co-citation analysis of information science, 1972-1995. *Journal of the American Society for Information Science*, 49(4), 327–355. 13

Wiener, N. (1948). *Cybernetics: or Control and Communication in the Animal and the Machine*. Cambridge, MA: MIT Press. 30

Wilson, T. D. (2006). Evolution in information behavior modeling: Wilson's model. In Fisher, K., Erdelez, S., and McKechnie, L. (Eds.), *Theories of Information Behaviors* (31–36). Medford, NJ: Information Today. 36

Xu, K., Ba, J., Kiros, R., Cho, K., Courville, A., Salakhudinov, R., and Zemel, R. S. (2015). Show, attend and tell: Neural image caption generation with visual attention. In *Proceedings of the 32nd International Conference on Machine Learning*, Lille, France. JMLR: W&CP, 37, 2048–2057.

Yarbus, A. L. (1967). *Eye Movements and Vision*. New York, NY: Plenum Press. DOI: 10.1007/978-1-4899-5379-7. 61, 67, 68, 69, 77, 82

Yoon, J. W. (2009). Toward a user-oriented thesaurus for non-domain-specific image collections. *Information Processing and Management* 45, 452–468. DOI: 10.1016/j.ipm.2009.03.004. 30, 32 , 40

Yoon, J. W. (2010). Utilizing quantitative users' reactions to represent affective meanings of an image. *Journal of the American Society for Information Science and Technology*, 61(7), 1345–1359. DOI: 10.1002/asi.21342. 38, 41

Yoon, J. W. (2011a). A comparative study of methods to explore searchers' affective perceptions of images. *IR Information Research*, 16(2). 38, 41

Yoon, J. W. (2011b). Searching images in daily life. *Library & Information Science Research*, 33, 269–275. DOI: 10.1016/j.lisr.2011.02.003. 52, 53

Yoon, J. W. and Chung, E. (2011). Understanding image needs in daily life by analyzing questions in a social Q&A site. *Journal of the American Society for Information Science and Technology*, 62(11), 2201–2213. DOI: 10.1002/asi.21637. 36, 37, 41

Yong, R., Huang, T. S., and Chang, S. (1999). Image retrieval: Current techniques, promising directions, and open issues. *Journal of Visual Communication and Image Representation* 10, 39–62. Available at: https://pdfs.semanticscholar.org/d700/824b23c3e42a5bbb-25413fa572b054750fd8.pdf. (accessed May 23, 2017). DOI: 10.1006/jvci.1999.0413.

Zeng, M. L., Gracy, K. F., and Žumer, M. (2014). Using a semantic analysis tool to generate subject access points: A study using Panofsky's Theory and two research samples, presented at the *International ISKO Conference*, May 19–22, 2014, Krakow, Poland. 34, 40

Authors' Biographies

Susanne Ørnager and Haakon Lund are colleagues at the University of Copenhagen as faculty members in the Department of Information Studies. Since 2014, they have presented courses about user tagging and digital image collections.

Susanne Ørnager obtained her Ph.D. in Computer Linguistics in 1999 from Copenhagen Business School (CBS), Denmark. From 1999–2012, she was Adviser for Communication & Information (CI) in Asia and the Pacific at the United Nations Educational, Scientific and Cultural Organization (UNESCO). Since 2012, she has taught courses in academic image organizations, social media and information methods, and information architecture and image management. She has published internationally in peer-reviewed academic outlets, presented research internationally to both academic and commercial audiences, participated in conferences and workshops, and served on review committees for humanities programs in the U.S.

Haakon Lund is currently an associate professor at the University of Copenhagen in Information Science. He has been working with the application of eye-tracking technology for a number of years and his research is primarily focused on the evaluation of information systems. He teaches courses on information architecture including the development of metadata schemas.